THE OUTDOOR CHUMS

Or

The First Tour of the Rod, Gun and Camera Club

Captain Quincy Allen

The Outdoor Chums

Captain Quincy Allen

PO Box 2211
Fairfield, IA 52556
www.1stworldlibrary.com
First Edition

LCCN: 2006907726

Softcover ISBN: 1-4218-2449-3
Hardcover ISBN: 1-4218-2349-7
eBook ISBN: 1-4218-2549-X

1st World Library Literary Society

Giving Back to the World

"If you want to work on the core problem, it's early school literacy."

- James Barksdale, former CEO of Netscape

"No skill is more crucial to the future of a child, or to a democratic and prosperous society, than literacy."

- Los Angeles Times

Literacy... means far more than learning how to read and write... The aim is to transmit... knowledge and promote social participation."

- UNESCO

"Literacy is not a luxury, it is a right and a responsibility. If our world is to meet the challenges of the twenty-first century we must harness the energy and creativity of all our citizens."

- President Bill Clinton

"Parents should be encouraged to read to their children, and teachers should be equipped with all available techniques for teaching literacy, so the varying needs and capacities of individual kids can be taken into account."

- Hugh Mackay

CONTENTS

CHAPTER I

PLANNING THE CAMPAIGN

"Great news, Jerry! The storm last night damaged the roof of the academy so that it has been condemned as unsafe. And the Head has decided that there can be no school held for two weeks."

"So Watkins was just telling me. He says most of the outside students are to be sent home again until repairs can be made. And I was just thinking that while I'm sorry for the Head, it opens up a jolly good prospect for some of us."

"How's that, Jerry? For myself, I was just feeling glad to be back at my desk again, after vacation, and now it's knock around again."

"All right, just stop and consider. There are four boys I know of, constituting the Rod, Gun and Camera Club, who have been busy planning an outing for next summer, back of the lumber camps at the head of the lake. Talk to me about opportunities, what's to hinder us going into the woods right now, and making use of our rods, guns, and that elegant new camera your mother gave you on your birthday last week?" demanded the boy called Jerry.

"What's all this about, you two conspirators?" demanded one of two other boys, swinging alongside just then, as though sure of a hearty welcome, and a voice at the council fire.

"Glad you came, Frank and Bluff, for I want your opinion. Jerry has just sprung an astonishing idea on me, and I'm so dazed I hardly know what to say. Are you ready for the question? All in favor of spending the two weeks' additional vacation out in camp back of the lumbermen's diggings say ay!"

The two newcomers looked at each other as if trying to grasp the immensity of the proposition; then they pulled off their hats, and giving a shout threw them into the air while both roared the affirmative word:

"Ay!"

Jerry looked at Will, with a broad smile of delight on his face.

"Three against one - the motion is carried!" he declared, triumphantly.

"Oh! come, I wasn't opposed to it in the start, only you stunned me by such a sudden and glorious idea. We'll meet with some opposition at home, I expect; but where there's a will there's a way; and I move we make it unanimous!" Will Milton hastened to remark.

"Bravo! consider it carried; and just to think what a chance it will be for me to try out my new outfit!" exclaimed the fourth boy, he who had been called by the queer name of "Bluff" by one of his comrades; possibly because, being the only son of a prominent lawyer, Dick Masters may have been addicted to the habit of putting up a bold face even when his heart was weak.

Jerry looked at him rather superciliously at this remark, and threw up his hands in a manner to indicate discouragement.

"I'm genuinely sorry for the feathered and furry game of the woods when the Great Hunter breaks loose with that terrible pump-gun. Mighty little chance for anything to get away after *that* is leveled, and the Gatling opens fire," he remarked scornfully.

"Huh! it's all very well for you to talk that way, Jerry, because you happen to be a fine shot, and can bag your game the first clip; but what's a fellow going to do when he finds it difficult to hit a barn? I'd like to wager that with all your high-falutin' talk you do more execution among the poor game than comes to my share," answered Bluff, indignantly.

"Oh! well, have it your own way. I've tried my best to show you what a genuine sportsman should be like, always giving the game a fair chance. Didn't I induce you to quit fishing with that murderous gang-hook last summer; and when you did finally get a bass didn't you feel prouder than if you just '*yanked*' him in, perhaps caught on the outside of his gills with some of that deadly jewelry?" demanded Jerry, whose one hobby was the "square deal" in all that he undertook.

"I acknowledge the corn about the gang-hook; but that has nothing to do with an up-to-date, repeating shotgun, and other things such as modern campers use. I've kept posted, and I know what's going on. Some people seem to be asleep, and are just contented to do as their forefathers did. I'm progressive, that's what."

"Well, boys," Frank Langdon here broke in with, "suppose you postpone that old chestnut of a dispute until we're snug in camp; and let's talk about how the thing can be done. The first thing is to get consent at home."

"I don't believe we need fear any trouble there. Frank, you call us up on the 'phone in about an hour, and if everything's lovely and the goose hangs high we'll meet at my house and make definite arrangements," said Will, whose mother was a well-to-do widow, and seldom refused her idolized son any reasonable request.

"We could go on our motor-cycles, and have a wagon bring

the duffle along. If it started at a decent hour in the morning we'd be able to get in camp by the middle of the afternoon, and have things fixed fairly well for the first night," suggested Jerry, his eyes bright with anticipations of a delightful time ahead.

"You've got all the things needed, Frank; and now we'll see what your experience up in Maine amounted to. Say, ain't this just glorious? Think of it, two weeks' outing at this beautiful time of the year, and up there in the woods where we were just planning to go next summer. I wonder if old Jesse Wilcox has begun to set his traps yet; that's his stamping-ground, you know, during the winter, and he makes quite a haul of muskrats, 'coons, some mink and even an otter once in a long while," said Bluff, enthusiastically - he was always a leading spirit in new ventures, but lacked the pertinacity of Frank.

"Don't you worry, old fellow, I'll be Johnny-on-the-spot when it comes to delivering the goods. But all further talking had better be put off until we find out whether we can go or not. So I move we adjourn, to meet again an hour from now at Will's shack," remarked young Langdon, always logical.

They had stopped to talk the matter over alongside one of the stores in the town; and indeed Bluff was perched upon an empty box, that lay at the foot of a small pyramid of similar cases, piled up until such time as they could be sold or destroyed.

While the others were talking, Jerry had made a little discovery that aroused both his curiosity and his temper: he had seen a touseled head, surmounted by a cap he knew full well, push up a little above the rim of the most elevated empty box, as if some concealed listener might be endeavoring to hear better, and in his eagerness recklessly exposed himself in this way.

Jerry was always prompt about doing things, nor did he, as a rule, stop to figure what the immediate consequences might prove to be.

Indignation at the idea of their conference having been overheard possessed his soul, and, seeing a splendid chance to bring the plans of the listener to a sudden and disastrous end, he managed without warning to give one of the boxes a flirt with his hand that moved it out a foot or two.

As it happened to be the keystone of the arch, the consequence was the entire pile came tumbling down, much after the fashion of a crumbling church during an earthquake.

Bluff gave a wild shout, and sprang to a position of safety, to turn and stare in astonishment at the remarkable result of the catastrophe.

From under the ruins a figure came crawling slowly, rubbing sundry places about his legs and sides, where the sharp corners of the boxes had been in cruel contact with his flesh.

"Why, it's Andy Lasher!" exclaimed Jerry, pretending to be wonderfully surprised. "Where in the world did you come from - hiding in that drygoods box, eh? Up to some of your old tricks, Andy, I guess. Going to carry off the whole dry-goods emporium that time, perhaps?"

The boy managed to get upon his feet, though he continued to limp around and rub his legs vigorously, as he whistled to keep from groaning.

Andy Lasher was known as the town bully, and many a time had he taken delight in giving our four friends more or less trouble; Jerry and he had always been at loggerheads, and could look back to half a dozen occasions in the past where the contest for supremacy had brought them to the point of battle.

Each time Andy was supposed to have gotten the better of the conflict, though his friends thought he paid dearly for his victory; but Jerry seemed never to know when he was whipped, and was just as ready to try conclusions with the other as before.

"Some fine day I'll know how to outwit the big brute, and then I mean to cure him of his bullying ways," he was wont to say cheerfully, as he festooned his face with strips of adhesive plaster, and tried to grin through the pain.

"What d'ye mean upsetting me that way, Jerry Wallington? Think just because your dad's a big railroad man you can knock poor fellers around any old way? I guess I've got some rights. You might have killed me, tumbling that pile of boxes down, with me inside. You ought to be made to pay fur it, that's what," grumbled the fellow, scowling vindictively, and yet not daring to assume the offensive while the four chums were present; for he had never tried conclusions with Frank, and was suspicious of the new boy in Centerville - for the Langdons had lived there about a year, Frank's father having purchased the bank of which he was now president.

"How could I know anybody was hiding up there?" demanded Jerry, in pretended ignorance, though his eyes twinkled with humor as he watched the bully limping around and still rubbing his knee.

"Ain't I got a right to play hide-and-seek with my friends? Who told you to stop just underneath, and talk about campin' out up above the lumber docks? Think you're the whole team, do you? Well, perhaps you won't shout just so loud when you know me and some of my mates are going up in that region ourselves, to-morrow, to see old Bud Rabig, the trapper, and if we have any trouble with you sissies there's bound to be a high old mix-up, see?" and he glared first at one and then at each of the others in turn.

The boys looked at one another in dismay, for it seemed as though some would-be joker had tossed a bucket of ice-cold water over them; this vague threat of Andy Lasher's was not to be lightly dismissed as mere bluff, for whatever his reputation might be, the fellow had a way of keeping his word, especially when it concerned any sort of mischief.

Frank, however, laughed aloud.

"That sort of talk doesn't cut any figure with us, Lasher. If we go up to the head of the lake we'll try and mind our own business, and advise all others to do the same, if they know what's good for them. We're not out looking for trouble, but, if it comes along, you and your cronies will find that there are four fellows who know how to take care of themselves. Got that, Andy?" he said sternly.

The bully looked at him fixedly for a moment, and then drawing back his short upper lip after a way he had, and which made his face resemble that of a snarling wolf, with fangs exposed, he remarked:

"It makes me laugh to think of such a lot of tenderfeet in the woods. Be careful not to shoot yourselves, kids. Guns are mighty dangerous sometimes. And just make up your minds that we ain't agoing to be scared by big words. The fellows that train with me have been up against hard knocks too often to knuckle down before a lot of bluster and brag. Them two weeks'll be the liveliest you ever knew, take my word for it."

With his tongue in his cheek he scurried away, just in time to avoid the proprietor of the store, who now came bustling out to learn what all the racket might mean, and found our four boys busily replacing his pyramid of empty boxes.

CHAPTER II

READY FOR THE START

Centerville was a thriving town situated almost midway down the east shore of Camalot Lake, and very nearly opposite Newtonport on the opposite bank; in consequence, there was more or less rivalry between the two places, which condition extended from the shopkeepers and banks to the sports of the boys of the bustling miniature cities.

Since the four chums are to figure as the leading spirits in our stirring tales of the Outdoor Club, it seems only proper that we should take an early opportunity to introduce them more fully to the reader, together with some of their more prominent hobbies, hoping that the acquaintance thus begun may ripen into warm intimacy as we journey along in company.

Jerry Wellington's father was a railroad magnate, and in full sympathy with his boy's love for the open; indeed, it was from the elder Wellington that Jerry, no doubt, inherited his love for fair play, whether in games on the baseball or football arena, or in sports afield; his sympathies seemed to be always with the under dog in the fight, and he would scorn to shoot a rabbit or a quail unless in full flight; or to take a game-fish by any other means than the methods in vogue among true sportsmen.

On the other hand, Bluff Masters could never get it through

his head what need there was for all this fuss and feathers about giving the game a chance; he had the old primal instinct of the red Indian, whose one desire was to secure his quarry, no matter whether by hook or by crook; since Bluff never pretended to be anything of a shot, or an expert angler, perhaps he was right in believing that, so far as he was concerned, the game had all the chance necessary at any and all times.

Frank Langdon, as mentioned before, was the son of the banker, and having lived up in Maine knew about all there was to know about the tricks of campers; since his chums as yet had had only limited chances to discover what the extent of his knowledge might be, they were very anxious to put Frank to the test, and learn a few of the said wrinkles, calculated to make them better sportsmen.

Frank had one sister, a pretty girl named Nellie, and Bluff Masters had shown a decided partiality for her ever since they were first brought together.

The last one of the quartette, Will Milton, was one of the rich widow's two children, and since he and Frank were deeply interested in photography, it was perhaps only natural that Frank should be attracted by Will's twin sister, Violet, whom he believed to be the sweetest girl of his acquaintance.

These four boys attended the private school of Alexander Gregory, D.P., and the sudden announcement that during a recent storm the buildings had suffered so severely as to necessitate the closing of the academy for a limited period, had fallen upon the community like a thunderbolt from a clear sky.

Those students coming from a distance were being sent away at the expense of the proprietor of the school; and others, who belonged either in Centerville or Newtonport, were allowed to go home, subject to a call some two weeks later.

While the boys worked at replacing the fallen boxes, they kept up a running fire of observations regarding this new calamity that threatened their peace; for when Andy Lasher and the ugly crowd with which he trained took a notion to make themselves disagreeable they could do it "to the queen's taste," as Jerry said.

"Shall we give the outing up?" asked Frank, after he had heard some of the dire prophecies advanced by his comrades, especially Bluff Masters.

"Never!" exclaimed Jerry.

"Ditto!" cried Will, looking more determined than ever.

"Oh! I'm just as anxious to go as any one, only it seemed right to look the old thing squarely in the face before we started to lay plans. If the rest say go, you can count on me all right. I'm the last to squeal if trouble comes, and you know that, fellows," declared Bluff, glancing around defiantly.

It was a habit with Bluff to be always expecting something serious to happen; and in case his suspicions were verified, as might occasionally occur, he would crow over the others, and strut around as though he thought himself a prophet gifted with second-sight, and able to forecast coming events with ease.

On the other hand, should the prediction fail to come about there was always a good excuse handy to account for the failure.

"Well," said Frank, as he winked at Jerry, "since we are all of one mind, I don't know why we should waste any more time about it. For one, I'm going straight to the bank and have a friendly chat with my dad. I just feel dead certain he'll be as tickled over the chance of an outing as I am. He never forgets that he was a boy, you see. So-long, fellows; see you later at Will's house."

There was a scattering then and there, Bluff heading in the direction of the building where his father had his offices, while the other two kept on in company, their homes being close together.

Will was the only one who really expected any show of opposition: for his widowed mother simply idolized him, seeing every day new traits of character as well as little facial resemblances that made him appear more and more like the husband and father who was gone; but then the boy knew just how to overcome these scruples, and his arguments were always backed up by his twin sister, so that in the end he usually attained his wish.

His one great hobby lay in the line of photography, and such had been his remarkable success with a cheap outfit that his mother had surprised and delighted the boy on a recent birthday by giving him an expensive camera.

Of course, he was fairly wild to get away into the woods and secure many stunning pictures of the great outdoor folks, the birds and animals inhabiting the wilds. Will cared little about shooting, and expected to do all his hunting with his camera.

When about an hour later Frank called each of his chums up on the 'phone, and eagerly demanded to know how things had turned out, he was delighted to hear them say one after the other that everything was lovely, and full permission to go had been duly granted.

After lunch they held a grand pow-wow at the home of Will, to which the two girls were admitted; for it had been deemed best that all the schools in both Centerville and Newtonport should be closed for a few days, in order to make a few needed repairs after the storm.

"Frank, consider yourself appointed commander-in-chief; and now please tell each of us what we must do," said Will, as they gathered around in the living room.

"I'll see about the wagon that is to take our stuff up. One of us can meet the driver on the road after we've picked out the spot for the camp. Every fellow be sure to have his outfit ready at seven in the morning. Bring two blankets apiece, and the things I've written down here - a towel, soap, and such little necessities," returned Frank.

"Who looks after the grub part of it?" demanded Bluff, who was never known to be separated from his appetite.

"That's my part, too," said Frank; "only, if any of you have any particular fancy in the line of stuff to eat now's the time to add it to the list I've made out."

"Let's take a squint at it, partner," remarked Bluff, anxiously.

He ran through the list.

"Don't think I'm going on short rations," laughed Frank, noting the expression akin to dismay appearing on the other's face; "but you see we'll have our motor-cycles along, and when we need a new lot of groceries it'll just be fun to mount and fly down here to pick up a bundle. Read out the variety, Bluff, and see if any one thinks we want anything else."

"H'm, here's matches, sugar, tea, coffee, condemned milk - I mean condensed milk - butter, four loaves of bread made at home by Frank's hired girl, who's a dandy cook," read Bluff, in a sing-song tone. "Then comes bacon, salt pork for cooking fish with, half a ham, potatoes, pepper and salt, self-raising flour, cornmeal, fine hominy, rice, beans, canned corn, tomatoes, Boston baked beans, a jar of jam, canned corned-beef and crackers.

"What else - don't all speak at once?" asked Frank, holding a pencil ready.

"I say a nice juicy beefsteak for the first night in camp; we won't be able to produce any game at short notice, I reckon, and that would be fine; just put that down for my sake, chief," observed Jerry.

"And, say, ain't we going to have any onions?" asked Bluff indignantly, at which Frank doubled up as if taken with a fit.

"That's one on me, boys. Why, I wouldn't ever think of going into camp without a supply of good onions along. If you ever came trudging home at evening, with game on your back, tired to beat the band, and when near camp sniffed fired onions cooking, you'd say they're the best thing ever toted into the wilderness. That's the time you showed your good sense, Bluff, old man. Onions? Why, to be sure, and plenty of 'em. Anything more?" he laughed.

The boys shook their heads; they had not had enough experience in camping out to warrant suggesting other additions to the apparently complete list made by the fellow who had been there, and knew all about the needs of those who go into the wilderness.

"All right. If you happen to think of anything just get it, that's all. Look at Jerry grinning there. I bet I know what he's thinking about - that all this is utter foolishness, and that we ought to start out with nothing more than we could carry on our machines, and then takepot-luck? How about that?" demanded Frank.

"Oh! well, have it your own way, fellows," declared Jerry, with a shrug of his shoulders; "you know my ideas about these things. I'm the kind of a sportsman who goes into the woods as light as possible - give me a frying pan, coffee pot, tin cup and a pie platter, some pepper and salt, some matches, a camp hatchet to cut browse for my bed, and my trusty rifle with which to supply the game, and I warrant you I can get along as well as the fellow who makes a pack-horse of himself, and totes all sorts of canned goods over the carries."

"That sounds all mighty well in theory, but there's mighty

little practical sense about it. A blanket is the camper's best friend of a cool night; and even if he is lucky enough to shoot enough game to satisfy his wants, he'll get sick of one diet in a short time. I ought to know something about it, for I've tried it both ways," declared Frank.

"Yes," broke in Bluff at this juncture, "and you wait and see if Jerry don't eat his share of every blessed thing we pack in - he won't refuse one dish. He's quite satisfied to turn up his nose at others carrying loads, while he goes free; but, at the same time, he eats a quarter of the grub every time."

Both Frank and Will laughed heartily at this, in which they were joined by Nellie Langdon and Violet Milton.

"Pshaw!" scoffed Jerry, turning a bit red at the same time, "if others are silly enough to make pack-horses of themselves, and lug all such things into the primeval wilderness, why, of course, I'm willing to help dispose of them when the time comes; purely out of good-heartedness, you see, for it makes their loads lighter. Just drop that subject, boys, and put me down for a bottle of maple syrup; for when Frank gives us some of those famous flapjacks he's told about so often, we ought to have the proper thing to go with them."

So they talked the thing over from beginning to end, and it looked as if the team Frank expected to engage would have their work cut out for them, hauling all this camp stuff over the roads to the point beyond the head of the lake.

The boys were evidently eager to get to work, and hence the conference presently broke up, Jerry heading in one direction, and Frank and his sister, with Bluff finding some plausible excuse for hanging on, going in another.

Later on that day, while Frank was at the big grocery store, giving orders to have the various edibles put up so as to be ready on the following morning before seven o'clock, he was interested in seeing Andy Lasher, backed by several of his pals, actually making similar purchases, though just where they secured the necessary funds, having no rich fathers to appeal to, was somewhat of a mystery.

Andy sent many a dark look across at the tall boy he secretly feared, but apparently he knew that this was no time to bring matters to a head, and hence there was nothing said; but the look on his freckled face told of dark intentions.

CHAPTER III

THE RACE FOR A CAMP-SITE

"All aboard for Kamp Kill Kare!"

Frank Langdon jumped off his motor-cycle as he shouted these words, and there was a scurrying among the other three boys, who had gathered at the house of Will, which had been mentioned as a place of meeting.

Each motor-cycle had numerous small packages secured about it after the individual fancy of the owner. Will carried his precious camera over his shoulder, but the tripod, a folding affair of the latest patent, was tied to his wheel; Jerry and Frank had their guns securely cased, and so arranged that they would not interfere with either the working of the machine or any jumping on and off; while Bluff carried his new repeating shotgun hung from his back with a strap.

He saw Jerry eyeing the same with a sneer, and was up in arms immediately.

"Just you wait, and don't cry before you're hurt. This bang-up modern machine shooter is no more murderous for me than yours is in your hands. 'Sufficient unto the day is the evil thereof!' and I'm ready to compare notes at the end of our little expedition, to see who has slaughtered the most game," and Bluff wagged his round head with its thatch of yellow hair, defiantly.

"Well, a man is known by the company he keeps, and any true sportsman - " began Jerry, ready to open the discussion on the spot.

"Rats!" exclaimed Will, as he got in readiness to mount his machine; "stow all that hot air until the first chilly night. Perhaps you'll need it before long. I say, Frank?"

"Well, what?"

"Has the wagon started along?" asked the other, eagerly.

"Yes, I saw it off before coming over here. Everything's aboard, and unless old Uncle Toby has an accident on the road, he guarantees to get up there shortly after noon," replied the leader, quietly.

"So, you got your hired man to do the driving; and I've half a suspicion the team comes from your place, too. That's mighty nice of your father, Frank. Suppose we could keep Toby with us one night to see us started?"

"Father said we could have him all we wanted. He can take the horses over to the nearest farm, where we expect to get our supply of fresh eggs, and then do a part of the cooking for us, as well as chop wood and some other stunts that, say what you will, kind of pall on a fellow after a little while."

"Better and better," remarked Jerry, who had been known on occasion to flunk when it came to drudgery, and wanted to be fishing or roaming pretty much all the day, and every day.

"Well, the reason I asked was this: I wouldn't wonder but what Andy Lasher and his pals might plan to intercept our supplies, and do something mean to break up our fun," continued Will, earnestly.

"Whew! I hadn't thought of that," remarked Jerry, looking alarmed.

"I had, and I made an arrangement with old Uncle Toby to take Erastus along in the wagon up to the point where we are to meet him at noon. You know Erastus is the porter and watchman at the bank, and known to be a fighter. When they see him sitting there beside Toby those fellows will have business somewhere else, you mark me. He can come home on the late afternoon train, one of us taking him over to the little station on a motor-cycle. How does that suit you all around?"

"Talk about your Napoleon for laying out plans; it couldn't be better arranged. The supplies will be safe, then. Now, is there anything else to remember?" demanded Jerry.

"Not from me," replied Bluff, stealing a side glance at the open window where Nellie and Violet were standing, watching the starting of the wonderful expedition that was expected to startle the timid woods folks up beyond the lumber camps at the head of the lake.

"Count me out," declared Will, raising one foot to be ready to mount.

"That settles it, then. Who goes first?" asked Frank.

"You do, to start with. Later on, after we pass the wagon, Jerry will act as guide, as he's been up there before, and knows a lot about the country," called Will.

"Then, here goes, fellows."

Suiting the action to the word Frank ran with his machine, then gave a vault into the saddle, started the engine, and with a loud popping the motor-cycle began to hustle along the road at a moderately swift pace.

Jerry came second, then Will, and last but not least Bluff, who was very apt to have many things happen to his motor-cycle before the ten miles had been reeled off, for that seemed to be just his fortune.

"Good luck!" called the girls from the window; while the little mother waved a 'kerchief from the doorway, and then hurried in to shed a few tears, for, truth to tell, these partings always affected her in this way.

Through the town they went, with dogs racing alongside and barking wildly, and quite a few persons waving them good wishes as they passed; for it was pretty well known what the Outdoor Club had in view, and the hunting toggery with which Bluff had adorned himself was a constant sign as to the glut there would presently be in the game market of Centerville.

Then past Frank's home, where his father waved his hat as he stood in the doorway, warned of the coming of the squad by the rampant popping of the motor-cycles; and after that the open country, where the northbound road ran alongside the calm waters of Lake Camalot, now glistening in the frosty air of an October morning.

Frank slowed up to allow of Jerry overtaking him, so that they might talk as they covered the miles.

"There's the wagon ahead," he said.

"I had noticed it, and just beyond I thought I saw several fellows up on the bank, perhaps Andy and his chums. It might be well for us to close in and be ready to defend the wagon if necessary. And look out for any sort of sharp-pointed nails on the road, apt to slash our tires," remarked Jerry, who had experienced so much of the trickery of the Lasher crowd that he believed there was nothing too mean or small for them to attempt.

"Not a bad idea, so slow up until the other boys arrive. They may hardly feel like doing anything, now that we happen along."

"I'd feel sure they wouldn't if we could only coax Bluff to

exhibit that awful pump-gun of his. Talk about your scorchers, I think Andy would run a mile - I know I would if I thought the murderous thing was going to be turned on me," growled Jerry, who, as the reader must already have noticed, was a very persistent fellow, and hard to convince, especially when on his favorite subject of a fair deal for every living creature.

They moderated their speed, and passed the place where the hostile group stood, with two riders on either side of the supply wagon.

Then it was seen that Andy and his associates had impressed a hungry-looking, gaunt mule into their service, the said animal being fairly loaded down with an assortment of the most astonishing articles ever dreamed of in the mind of would-be campers.

Under the circumstances, with Erastus and Toby to help guard the camp outfit, Andy's crowd did not dare lift a hostile hand; but they took especial pains to hoot at the little company as it wheeled past, making more or less sarcastic remarks, and yet being careful not to go too far.

The truth was, they did not wholly like the looks of the big colored man who sat there with old Toby, and of whose abilities as a fighter they happened to know something about.

When the rival campers had been left far behind, the boys considered it safe to part company with the supply train, and dash off.

"We've got lots to do, locating on a good campsite, remember, fellows; those sort of things don't grow on every bush, I tell you; so, come along," and Frank, as he spoke, let out another kink, the popping grew more furious, and away he shot up the road in a little cloud of dust, with Jerry at his rear, ready to take the lead as soon as there was any necessity for choosing at the forks.

Ten miles is a mere "flea-bite," as Bluff Masters said, when a good, lively motor-cycle "takes the bit in its teeth," and it seemed as though they had hardly more than got well started before the junction was reached, where Jerry swung ahead, and the rest trailed after him.

The pace had to be more moderate after this, for the going was not so even; but, nevertheless, they made fair time, and finally swung around at the head of the lake, where the logging camp was situated.

It was early in the season, but there were some timber cutters at work in the woods near-by, and a greasy man-cook stood in the doorway of the long log cabin where the gang put up throughout the winter, while conducting their operations of leveling the forest, or, at least, robbing it of all the spruce for the pulp mill over at Bedington.

Jerry held up at the lumber camp, for he wished to ask a few questions of the cook, who was a man he happened to know in a small way, though never particularly fancying Jock Stovers.

The fellow stared at seeing a quartette of elegant motor-cycles come dashing up to the loggers' winter quarters.

"Hello! Jock. We're going into the woods to spend a week or two; wagon following after with all the stuff. Where do you suppose we could run across old Jesse Wilcox these days; and is he starting to do any trapping?" asked Jerry.

The lumber-camp cook grinned a little as he took in the new and striking hunting apparel which Bluff Masters sported so airily; doubtless he immediately concluded that the whole party must be a set of greenhorns, incapable of knowing enough to come in out of the wet when it rained.

"Oh! yes, he's to work, they tells me. Leastwise I heerd ole Bud Rabig complainin' thet he never did hev a show wen Jesse he was around, 'cause the annermiles they jest seem ter hanker arter Jesse's traps. Folks do say he hes a kinder scent he uses ter jest coax 'em like," replied the cook, not above hoping these sons of Centerville rich people might think it worth while to toss him a generous tip for any information he gave them.

"We are heading for that old camp by the twin hemlocks, where that spring bubbles up, winter and summer. One of us will be back here to convoy old Toby in with the chuck wagon, and get Erastus over the farmers' station, where he can catch a late train back. Just tell them to wait here, if they come before I arrive, and here's some tobacco money for your trouble, Jock."

The cook nimbly caught the flying coin, and grinned his thanks.

"Oh! I'll tell 'em all right, don't yer be 'fraid, Jerry. Say, they was a party o' three as started in ter camp jest whar ye say, about a hull hour ago. Boys from Centerville, too, but a tough-lookin' bunch. They tried to do me for a breakfast, but I come out with a gun, and they shooed. Reckon that Pet Peters was wun o' the gang."

"Whew!"

Jerry looked at the others in some dismay.

"What'll we do, fellows; that's Andy's right bower. He must have started the three of them up here last night, meaning to have them squat by the spring first, and keep us off. And I did want to camp just there above all places! It's been on my mind all night," exclaimed Jerry, disconsolately.

"An hour, you said, Jock?" asked Frank, always quick to decide knotty points.

"I reckons about that; but them fellers was dog-tired, an' I don't think they's agoin' ter git up to thet spring in a hurry," replied the cook, still squeezing the half dollar, as if to "make it squeal," as Bluff remarked later.

"Perhaps we can get there before they do. Suppose we make a try, Jerry?"

For answer Jerry started his machine on a run, jumped aboard, and was quickly dashing away at rather a reckless pace, considering the rough "tote" road he had to follow.

The others were close at his heels, and altogether the rattling reports of the four exhausts quite excited the lumber-camp cook, who stood there in the doorway gaping, as long as the motor-cycles remained in sight.

CHAPTER IV

UNDER THE TWIN HEMLOCKS

"Say, ain't this going-some, for a rough road?" called Bluff, who was pounding along close behind Jerry, Will bringing up the rear.

"Beats everything I ever did on wheels - wow! that was a scorcher of a jolt! I hope none of the wheels break down!" answered the other, over his shoulder; but he dared not take his eyes off the uneven "tote" road which they were following, for more than a second at a time, lest some unfriendly root hurl him into the ditch, a wreck.

"See anything of 'em, Frank?" wheezed Jerry a bit later, as he kept his machine close behind the leader; for somehow in this race for the campsite Frank just naturally forged to the front from mere force of habit.

"Thought I had a peep of something moving ahead - soon know," came the answer.

Some more jumping followed, and it required considerable agility on the part of the four riders to keep their saddles.

Then they made a turn, and discovered three boys in full flight ahead.

"There they are!" cried Jerry, in excitement.

"How far ahead is the spring?" called Frank.

"About half a mile, I reckon."

"Good! Then the game is ours, barring accidents!"

The three fellows ahead kept turning around every dozen seconds, as if worried at the rapid approach of the others.

"Keep your eyes peeled; they're hatching up some sort of mischief!" called Frank, who knew the signs.

He saw that the others began to wobble in their movements, which was plain evidence that they had tired themselves out by their night tramp, and were in no condition to compete with the motorcycles, even on this rough stretch of road.

The tall, athletic-looking leader of the trio suddenly jumped aside, and stooped over as if snatching something from the ground.

"'Ware, hawks!" shouted Bluff, who had noted this maneuver.

It could now be easily seen that Pet Peters had fastened upon quite a cumbersome branch of a fallen tree, and his purpose was manifest when he stepped out as if to drop it across the road, meaning to wreck the machines as they swept on.

Frank changed his course just a trifle, but was now heading straight for the unprincipled schemer, who would have taken the chances of seriously injuring some of the party in order to further his own plans.

The sight of that heavy motor-cycle heading straight at him rather demoralized Pet, who did not know but that Frank meant to chase him until he got him; so that he dropped the branch before he had quite covered the entire space across the narrow road, and made a wild leap for safety.

Consequently, Frank was able to veer aside and skim past the dangerous obstruction without coming a "cropper" in the ditch.

Jerry also swept by, and the others were coming so fast on the heels of the two leaders that the bewildered roughs could not pull their wits together in time to make any successful swoop.

Perhaps they were not particularly anxious to arouse the party after all; for the sight of the weapons they carried, and, above all, the martial appearance of the khaki-clad Bluff, must have impressed them more than a little.

"Hurrah! the camp is ours!" yelled the tail-ender, as he clung to the rear of the remarkable procession; for never before had these solemn woods witnessed anything like such a progressive picture of modern magic as these four lads booming along on metal steeds capable of making fifty miles an hour and more, in case of necessity, and over a smooth road.

A few minutes later of more moderate traveling brought them to a point where a view could be had of the camp-site.

"Over to the right - notice those twin hemlocks yonder - well, the wonderful spring bubbles up close beside those trees. Hold up, Frank!" called Jerry.

So the quartette dismounted, jumping from their wheels while still in motion, after the habit of those who use motor-cycles.

In another minute all of them were bending low over the spring, testing the delightfully clear waters of the same.

Loud were the exclamations of satisfaction that arose, for their ride had made them thirsty, and the water was as cold as ice.

"A cracking good spot for a camp," was the verdict of the experienced Frank, as he allowed his eyes to rove about, and take in the surroundings.

Jerry beamed with pleasure.

"Knew you couldn't help liking it, for it seemed to cover all the necessities of the case, as far as I know them," declared Jerry, whose knowledge was founded pretty much on theory based on extensive reading rather than a practical experience such as Frank had passed through.

"This little knoll will serve to shed water when it rains, as it's sure to do some time or other; it always does when you camp; and the water is just far enough away to keep the spring from being polluted by any refuse from the fire. Yes, and the trees around here have not been touched by lumbermen, so that the whole aspect is restful to the eye. I like it, Jerry; it's a regular jim-dandy place."

"Hunk, I say!" declared Bluff, after his usual explosive fashion; but if his manner was crude, he generally hit the nail on the head, and no one could mistake his feelings in the matter.

He immediately squatted down and began to take his gun out of its case, an operation Jerry eyed with alarm.

"Say, look here, what are you going to do with that machine, eh? Are you so wild to get at the slaughter that you can't wait a decent length of time, and give the poor birds and beasts a chance to know we're here for a long stay? For goodness' sake, show some sportsman spirit, Bluff," he exploded.

The other looked up with an injured expression.

"Why," said he, "I'm only thinking of those three desperate characters rushing our camp, and I wanted to let them see we are able to look out for ourselves, that's what."

"Oh! if that's the case, hold up that tool, and I bet they light out faster than they come - who wouldn't, I'd just like to know, when - "

"Hey, Jerry, can the wagon get in here?" asked Will, knowing what the dispute would lead to if allowed to go on any further.

"Why, yes, I think so, if Toby knows how to manage right; you see he can turn to the right, cross behind that thicket, and bring up here; certainly the wagon can haul up here - if it ever gets to this point safe," replied the other.

"You and I will look out for that, and when we ride back to convoy it here, depend on it, we'll have our guns ready to make a good showing," remarked Frank. "I don't think those three fellows will dare attack us, especially when they see Erastus. They know him all right, from sad experience. You see 'Rastus used to be something of a prizefighter in a small way among his kind, and nothing delights him half so much as a scrap once in a while; and the town rowdies have suffered at his hands."

"All right; say when, and I'll be ready to go."

"Plenty of time. I figure that the wagon won't get to the lumber camp until noon, so in the meantime we can be using that nice ax Will has strapped to his machine, and doing a number of things. Firewood is a mighty handy article to have around a camp, boys, and it's simply wonderful what a big lot of it is needed."

"A hint is as good as a command, Frank; just understand that we're ready to do anything you suggest, for we all want to learn the ropes as soon as we can. What are you going to do?" he asked, as Frank unsheathed a camp hatchet, and commenced to look around, as if in search of some particular kind of wood.

"Well, you see, I remember that I lost my tent pegs the last time I camped in Maine, and it's up to me to cut a new supply. No better time than now, while we're waiting for the wagon. Then I expect to lay out several poles on which to stretch the tents - one tall one for the center, and a couple of others outside for the fly that forms a shelter," remarked

Frank, commencing operations on what seemed a suitable piece of hickory.

"What sort of tents are they?" asked Jerry, watching all that the other did, so as to catch the true spirit of the thing from practical observation, which somehow seemed vastly different from what he read in his books on sport.

"The kind which most canoeists like in these modern days. They're big enough to accommodate four in a pinch, although it's much better to have only two in each, and that's why I brought both along. Then, when the fly in front is raised it makes a splendid place for the table, being sheltered from sun and rain. Each tent has a waterproof floorcloth, to keep the dampness out. Wait and see, Jerry."

They worked like beavers for a time.

When one tired his muscles chopping firewood another was eager to take up the job, and it was wonderful how the pile of fuel increased.

Frank rubbed his hands with pleasure when, an hour or more later, he came over to take a look at it, having completed his own task, as the quantity of tent pegs announced.

"That's fine, fellows" he declared, laughing. "If you'd ever gone through what I did once, when lost in the Maine woods one bitter cold night, you'd never think you could have too big a pile of the stuff. Perhaps some time I'll tell you about that experience; for I'll never forget it, never. But, Jerry, suppose we get ready to run back to the lumber shack, and wait there for the wagon? I won't be easy until we see it here. A little snack first from the grub I've got here, and which Nellie put up for us, and then we'll meander over the back trail," he said.

"Grub!" exclaimed Bluff, starting up from the soft, mossy cushion he had fashioned, after doing his little stunt with the ax; " count me in, please, and especially if your sister put it up,

Frank, for I reckon it must be the boss feed then."

At which the others smiled, for Bluff's weakness regarding Frank's pretty sister was something of a joke among them.

But when the package was undone there were broad grins, for dainty sandwiches flanked by a generous assortment of wings and drumsticks, connected at one time with a number of spring chickens, came into view, besides some pickles, and even a bunch of cookies, which Frank assured his chums had been actually made by the fair hands of Nellie herself.

They had hardly known just how hungry they were until the first bite was taken, and then little was said for some time, on account of the rapidity with which those four sets of sturdy jaws worked.

But, as might have been expected, Bluff was the first one to reach out his hand and secure one of the aforesaid cookies, which he munched with closed eyes, as if mentally picturing the sweet girl from whom the treat had come.

"All ready for the road, Jerry!" exclaimed Frank, jumping up.

"On deck, captain; I'm with you," came the reply, just as cheerily.

"You fellows keep a good watch, though I don't fancy you'll be bothered by the three advance scouts of the Lasher brigade," remarked Frank, as he pushed his machine into position, and prepared to run with it for a start.

"Huh!" grunted Jerry, casting a side glance toward Bluff, who was already shifting his repeating shotgun to a position where it could lie across his knees as he sat there on his mossy hassock; "I bet they won't, not as long as that thing is in sight. Talk about your scarecrows, I'd like to wager - "

"To be continued in our next; come along, Jerry," cried Frank, as he started on.

A minute later the merry popping of the two exhausts told that the convoy for the "chuck-wagon," as they called it, was on the way.

CHAPTER V

THE FIRST CAMP SUPPER

"They don't seem to be around," said Jerry, when he and his chum had covered at least half the distance to the lumber camp, without seeing a sign of the three fellows who had tried to dispute their advance in the morning.

"I hope they're not hovering around our camp, to make trouble for the boys," observed Frank, shaking his head.

The other laughed aloud in a scoffing way.

"All I can say is, I'm mighty sorry for Pet and his pals if they try that sort of business when that criminal of a Bluff is sitting there with his Gatling gun, ready for work. I'd sooner face a tiger, honest I would, than that instrument of destruction. I bet there won't be a chippy left around here when we get out."

"Oh! shucks, Jerry, remember that he isn't in your class. When he empties that six-shot gun and makes a miss every time, what does it matter? If the game had only poor Bluff and his repeater to fear they could well laugh. But when *you* look over the sights it's a different matter."

"That's nice of you, Frank. I'll try and be more lenient with the poor fellow, then. Anyhow, I know he shuts both eyes when he pulls the trigger, for I've watched him more than once. A man that's gun-shy never will make a success as a hunter. Isn't that so?"

"I've been told so; but, all the same, Bluff is a good-hearted chap, and I like him first rate. He furnishes fun for the whole squad; and, besides, nothing makes him mad - at least, if he ever brushes up it's over and done with like a flash. But isn't that the lumber camp ahead - I thought I had a glimpse of it through the trees - there it is again!" said Frank.

"You're right, but I don't see the wagon."

"I hardly thought it would be here before half an hour more. We needn't go any farther than the cabin, and can be taking in the sights while we wait."

"Precious little to see here; don't compare with some of the big camps up in your Maine, I guess. But they're making a gash in the timber all right, and in a few years it'll be all gone - that is, what is worth taking."

They came to a halt near the log cabin, from which the head of the cook was quickly thrust, he having heard the sound of their engines as they approached.

"Back again, boys?" he inquired genially, for the vision of that coin was still fresh in his memory.

"Bad penny always comes back, Jock," laughed Jerry.

"We've come to convoy the wagon in. You see all our supplies, tents, grub and blankets happen to be in that wagon, and we don't mean to let it be captured by any of the Lasher crowd," remarked Frank.

He saw the cook start at the mention of that name, as he muttered:

"Butch Lasher a-comin' up hyer - then them fellers must aben some o' his pals."

"Just what they were," and Frank went on to explain how it came there was a second vacation for the academy boys of Centerville, and also the unfortunate fact of Andy, known among his chums as "Butch" for some unexplained reason, having determined to take an outing in the same region at the identical time they had arranged to come.

"We expect to have trouble with them right along, but they'd better be careful how they try any of their smart tricks on us up here. We mean to let them alone, if they mind their business and pay no attention to us; but, on the other hand, we know how to defend ourselves, and we've got the means to do it," he went on.

The cook shook his touseled head.

"Thet critter is sure a terror, an' I orter know," was all he would say; but the boys could imagine that there was some sort of a story back of it.

Less than ten minutes later, while Jerry was prowling around looking at the bunks in which the lumberjacks slept when in camp, the sound of voices came to Frank, who was watching outside, and looking down the crooked road he caught sight of the wagon, with the two colored men on the seat.

A shout brought Jerry plunging out of the door, and he joined in noisilygreeting the coming of the team.

It had been previously arranged that he was to take Erastus on his machine over to the station on the railroad, about two miles away, so that he might get the afternoon local, which would stop upon being flagged.

Meanwhile, Frank would escort the wagon to the camp, feeling quite able to take good care of the supply train, as Jerry called it, when he tired of saying "chuck-wagon."

Jerry got away first, with Erastus perched behind him, and

grinning from ear to ear with the novelty of the experience.

"H'm, he won't think it so funny if they strike a root and take a header; but then Jerry's a cautious driver, and he knows something of the lay of the land; so I hope they'll get along without a spill. Now, Uncle Toby, do you think you can stand a mile or two of rough sledding; for the 'tote-road' is hardly meant for a wagon with springs?" Frank asked, as the other vanished from sight, going back along the way they had come from Centerville.

"'Deed an' I specks I kin, Marse Frank; dis chile is able to stan' a heap o' knockin' 'round on 'casion. S'long as I keeps my shins safe, I don't seem to keer 'bout much else. Say de word, sah, an' I'se ready to hit um up ag'in right peart," was the reply from the old, gray-headed Toby, who had worked for Frank's father many years - indeed, he was fond of saying he had been a slave in the Virginia branch of the Langdon family "befo' de wah."

The horses had not had a very hard pull up to this time, and were, therefore, in pretty fair condition to attempt the last quarter of the journey.

And they needed all their strength to drag that heavily-laden wagon over the half-broken road, where so many obstacles stuck up to jolt the poor driver until he almost lost his grip on the seat, though the boys had been able to avoid most of these because they could steer aside with the single line of wheels.

But the vehicle had been well made, and the horses were full of vim,while the venerable black man who gripped the reins was a "sticker," as he expressed it, after being once tossed out upon the back of the near horse by the sudden stoppage of the wagon.

After rather a trying experience they finally sighted a column of smoke, and, calling Toby's attention to this, Frank said:

"That's as far as we go this time, Toby."

Toby shut his eyes for a brief moment and doubtless gave thanks, for his poor old body must have been pretty well bruised by this time.

Will and Bluff had spied the wagon by now, and they shouted a noisy welcome.

"Now we're prepared for a siege, with the grub at hand," cried Bluff, dancing around with his gun held on high.

"Say, be careful with that contraption, will you? If ever it started going off not one of us would live to tell the ghastly tale," called Will, as if really and truly alarmed, which, of course, he was not.

Bluff gave him an indignant look, for it pained him to have his pet gun insulted after this rude fashion; but he was too much delighted over the coming of the supply wagon to cherish any animosity; and besides, as Frank said, he never could keep on being angry over a few minutes at a time.

Such fun they had getting that vehicle unloaded.

Then the tents had to go up, which was an operation that consumed considerable time, for Frank proved to be very exact in his way of arranging things, and would not accept any poor work.

When finally both tents had been erected, with a burgee bearing the club name floating from the very tops, the camp began to have a mighty cheery look that was invigorating.

Then another fly was put up just in the rear, under which some of the coarser provisions, such as water would not injure should the rain get in, were stored; here, too, Toby was to bunk while in camp.

"Everything looks like business, boys," said Jerry, as he came in later.

"What did you do with Erastus?" demanded Frank; "upset him in a ditch?"

"Do I look like I had been rooting? He got off on the train, and is home by now."

Home - the boys looked at each other, for it already seemed as though they had been away a long time, and yet their first night under canvas was still ahead.

They meant to keep the horses with them over night, and next day Jerry would go with Toby to the farmer's, about a mile off, leaving the outfit there until it was needed to take them back again.

As evening came on the boys began to lie around and watch the old darkey start operations for supper, which he did with evident delight; for Toby loved nothing better than to get away with "Marse Frank" and some of his friends, where he could wait upon them and enjoy a holiday in the woods.

The unusual exertions of the ride and subsequent wood-chopping had really tired all of the chums, though none of them would publicly admit it. When Bluff attempted to get up in a hurry for some purpose, he found himself so stiff he could hardly move, and it was only after much grunting and three distinct efforts that he finally managed to reach his feet.

Frank only smiled.

He had expected just this, and knew that in a few days the boys would have succeeded in getting the kinks out of their muscles.

Bluff had insisted that they have fried onions with that glorious steak, and, indeed, he even prepared a dozen of the same himself, for Bluff could be very persistent when he chose; Frank called a halt at this number.

"We may want a few another time, old fellow," he admonished.

"Oh! all right, then. I was just waiting till somebody called me off. I've shed more tears than Brutus ever dropped at the bier of Caesar. Wow! some kind person wipe my eyes, please; my hands are too rank to touch my tear-rag," he declared, and Will performed this friendly office, thinking that he deserved it after his heroism.

The coffee was soon bubbling on the fire, and the delightful odor of that fine sirloin steak, together with a second frying-pan full of onions, so permeated the surrounding atmosphere that had any of the Lasher crowd been hiding in the vicinity they must have suffered tortures in the thought that they were debarred from that glorious outdoor feast around the first campfire.

"Look there!" said Jerry, quietly, pointing as he spoke.

"It's a little chipmunk come to find out what all this row is about here," remarked Frank, tossing a piece of bread toward the cunning animal. "If you don't do anything to frighten them away we can have a lot of such friendly creatures hanging around the camp all the time."

"Then, for goodness' sake, chain up that annihilator of Bluff's before he gets it working overtime. Looks as if he had an eye on it just now, for game is game to the pot hunter, no matter how he gets it, or what it happens to be," growled Jerry, scowling in the direction of the other, who only grinned in reply.

"Supper am ready, gemmen. Kindly draw yer seats 'round de table," announced the tow-headed cook at this juncture; and in the eagerness to appease their keen hunger everything else was forgotten for the time being.

Two collapsible tables had been brought along, and these were placed under the raised fly of one of the tents, so that the warmth of the open fire could be enjoyed; but the whole supper had not been cooked after the old fashion, for Frank had a little outfit that burned kerosene, making its own blue flame, and which the other boys declared to be the finest thing of the kind they had ever seen.

A set of aluminum ware went with it, the kettles nesting in each other; there were cups, dishes, knives, forks and spoons for four persons; besides, Frank had added a lot of kitchen things from the house, so that they were amply supplied.

The supper was almost finished when something crashed through the branches of a tree and fell at Frank's feet.

"What's that?" exclaimed the boy.

Crash! came another object. It landed on a platter and bounded off into Bluff's lap.

"A rock! Somebody is throwing rocks at us!" cried Will, starting to scramble to his feet in wild excitement.

"It must be one of that Lasher crowd," ejaculated Jerry; "come on, boys, and let's get hold of the fellow!"

CHAPTER VI

BLUFF MEETS WITH A LOSS

The wildest excitement ensued.

Jerry met with a mishap right in the beginning of the hunt, falling over the long box in which much of their camp material had been carried.

It happened to lie just back of the tent, empty save for a few fag-ends of canvas brought along in case of need, and with the cover in place.

"Talk about your obstacle races!" he shouted, as he scrambled up, and went limping after the others; "this has 'em beaten to a frazzle."

The hunt for the offender was without result. He had evidently made haste to scuttle off, after heaving the stones at the camp.

Frank and Will, after searching for some little time, started to return to the camp, and on the way overtook Bluff.

"Where's Jerry?" asked Frank, as they joined forces.

"Don't know," came the answer, as Bluff pushed on eagerly ahead; "last I saw of him he was taking a header over that long coffin-box back of the tents."

"I hope he didn't hurt himself badly, that's all. What's your hurry, Bluff?" continued Frank, noticing that the other seemed particularly anxious to get along.

"Why, I left my gun standing against a tree," replied Bluff.

"Well, we all did about the same thing. I forgot I had a gun, in fact, being so anxious to get my hands on that chump who bombarded our camp. I guess you'll find the gun safe. Uncle Toby stayed in camp," said Frank, nudging Will.

"He did not. I saw him scooting off like a scared dog. Like as not that coon is hiding somewhere under the bushes at this very minute," declared Bluff.

At which both the others laughed.

Presently the cheery blaze was seen through the trees.

Some one was there, for they could see him bending over as though busily engaged.

"It's Jerry, all right," said Bluff, over his shoulder.

"But what in the wide world is he doing? I believe he's been hurt, boys," declared Frank, with a touch of anxiety in his voice, for Jerry and he had been very thick of late.

"Binding a bandage around his shin, as sure as you live! Hello! What happened to you, old fellow? Did one of those rocks hit home, or was it the box you tried to capture that jumped up and kicked you?" asked Will.

Bluff was in the meantime rushing wildly about the camp as though looking for something.

"I tumbled over that plagued box, that's all; and after limping around for a spell thought I'd better come back and put some witch-hazel on the bruise," explained the other, turning down his trousers' leg, and scrambling to his feet to ascertain how well he could walk.

"It will be some stiff in the morning, I reckon. Talk about your bears, I thought one had me nailed when I fell over that thing 'ker chunk,'" he continued, as he rubbed his shin and screwed his face up as if to conceal his pain.

"I told you so - it's gone!" shouted Bluff, at this juncture.

"What's gone?" echoed Will.

"My gun! Something seemed to tell me it was a silly thing for me to run off in that way and leave it. And now they've stolen it!" wailed Bluff.

"What! Do you really mean to say you can't find it?" questioned Frank.

"Help me look, fellows. Oh! my heart will be broken if it's true. I was just dreaming of what great things I meant to do with that splendid repeating shotgun. Please search around the camp!" pleaded Bluff.

Of course they immediately started a thorough hunt for the strangely missing weapon, even the limping Jerry seeming as deeply interested in the search as any one of his comrades.

High and low they looked, turning over all the blankets in the tents, but not a sign of the wonderful "pump-gun" could they discover.

The other guns were just where they had been left, and so far as they could see not another thing had been stolen.

"I declare, this is mighty queer," remarked Frank, when they were ready to give over the quest.

"Strangest thing I ever heard of," declared Will.

"Talk about your airships, I think the blooming old thing must have taken wings and sailed away," grunted Jerry, still rubbing his wounded shin sympathetically.

"But why should they pick out Bluff's gun of the lot?" demanded Frank.

"That's easy enough to answer. They knew a good thing when they saw it, I bet that crowd noticed what a bully gun I carried, when we passed them on the road, and they've been hanging around ever since," avowed Bluff, positively.

"Then the rocks - " began Will

"Were fired at us only to tempt a rush. It was all a plot, fellows, to coax us away for a short time. And the worst of it is the game worked only too well. I'll never get over that loss, never! I feel sick!" went on Bluff.

He kept shaking his head as if working himself up into a desperate frame of mind. Evidently it would have gone hard with any one of Andy Lasher's crowd if the offended boy could have laid hands on him just then.

"I wonder if Uncle Toby could give us any information on this subject?" suggested Frank.

"Oh! call him in and see. Perhaps he even grabbed it up in his fright. Shout to him, Frank, please," exclaimed Bluff, eagerly.

"Hello! Uncle Toby! Show up here; the coast is clear, and all danger past!"

Placing his hands about his mouth, after the fashion of a megaphone, Frank shouted these words several times.

"There he comes!" cried Will, pointing to a moving object.

"Has he got anything in his hands?" gasped Bluff, anxiously.

"Not that I can see," replied the other.

Bluff groaned and wrung his hands disconsolately.

"It's gone, boys! I'll never set eyes on that beauty again. Might as well give up and go back to town," he said, gloomily, as if brokenhearted.

"Oh! shucks! Don't give up so easy, Bluff. Who knows but that we may find a chance to recover the gun again, sooner or later. Live in hopes."

"It's easy for you to say that, Frank, when your gun is all safe and sound. Why, what can I do now without anything to shoot game with?"

"Well, I wouldn't worry about that. This is Kamp Kill Kare, you know. Trust us to find plenty for you to do. There'll be fish and game to clean, and dishes to wash while Toby is busy at something else. Oh! you can be useful all right, I give you my word, Bluff," said Frank, gaily.

The aggrieved boy gave him one indignant look. He did not seem in a humor to trust himself to speech.

Meanwhile the aged darkey had entered the camp.

"Have you seen my repeating-gun, Toby?" demanded Bluff, striding up to him.

"'Deed an' I hasn't seen any gun since I jumped into de bush to find dem young raskils wot trowed dat stone at me. I war just a-wishin' I had a gun along. Wouldn't I jest a peppered dem scalawags as dey run past me?" replied the old fellow.

"Say, did you see them then?" demanded Frank.

"I shore did, Marse Frank."

"How many were there?" came the quick question.

"I war jest a-countin' ob dem jailbirds, an' had 'rived at 'leven w'en a 'streperous root she keeled me ober. W'en I gits up agin dey had gone. Den I heard Marse Frank a-callin' me to come back," went on Toby, glibly.

The boys looked at each other and smiled. They knew that without doubt he had been cowering close to the ground in mortal fear the whole time, for Uncle Toby had little reputation for bravery.

"Did you see any of them have a gun?" asked Bluff, faintly.

"I done t'ink de whole bunch hab guns; least-way dat was my 'pression at de time dat creeper done trip me up. It's lucky my haid is 'customed to hard knocks, or it split open for sure."

"That settles it; my new gun is gone. Oh! it makes me so mad just to think one of that crowd may be handling it," cried Bluff, shaking his fist.

"I just fancy I can hear the squirrels laughing, and the little chippies singing for joy," declared Jerry. "Now they'll have a chance to live. What's hard on you, Bluff, is just happiness to them."

"You always did envy me the possession of that gun, and I know it, in spite of your sneers. You just thought I'd beat you out in making a record. Wait! I'm going to get that cracker-jack gun back again, some fine day," remarked Bluff, grimly.

And Frank, seeing that look of determination on his face, knew he meant it.

CHAPTER VII

THE SHACK OF THE MUSKRAT TRAPPER

"Wake up, everybody!"

Bang! bang! bang! went the big spoon on the frying pan Frank held.

As the others came crawling out of the tents they sniffed the air.

"Say, that bacon smells prime!" declared Will, smacking his lips.

"Hope you didn't forget about that mess of hominy I spoke about last night, Toby. Hominy's my great stand-by for breakfast. All right, I see it on the fire. Give me just five minutes. If it wasn't for that gun - "

"Talk about your Ambrosia, that Java sure has it knocked clean out," broke in Jerry. "Me for a quick-dressing act and then grub!"

Uncle Toby grinned, for he knew what appetites boys are apt to develop when in the woods, and, of course, he had made allowances.

They were soon gathered around the table and busy.

"What's the programme for to-day?" asked Frank, when the edge of their appetites had been taken away.

"First thing of all I want some snapshots of the camp in the morning sun. You can see that's the best time to get a good view. Now, just sit still, fellows, and let me do my little trick," said Will.

They assumed grotesque positions, but the photographer refused to stand for that.

"What d'ye think I want, a collection of freaks broken loose from the lunatic asylum? Here, you, Will, be dishing out some more bacon on to your plate; Frank, take up the coffee-pot and be helping Bluff. Uncle Toby, just look pleasant."

"Pretend you found my gun, and I was giving you half a dollar, Uncle Toby," remarked Bluff, quickly.

"Always thinking of that cheap, clap-trap affair," growled Jerry. "Goodness knows if we'll hear anything else from him all the time we're in camp. I declare I've half a notion - "

"To do what?" asked Frank, looking at him suspiciously.

Jerry only smiled and shrugged his shoulders.

"Now, hold your positions, fellows. Frank, lean a little forward, so your face stands out better; there, that's right. Toby, raise your head and point up as if you saw a bird in that tree. That's good, all right; it's over. Thank you!"

Will kept his position for a little while, and every few minutes seemed to find a chance to snap off another view. He evidently believed in getting a variety of the main subject of their outing - the home camp.

"I move we try and find old Jesse Wilcox this morning," suggested Frank.

"That suits me, if we don't have to go too far," agreed Jerry.

"How's the shin, by the way, this morning? Haven't noticed you limp much?"

"Feels pretty fair. Next time I chase out of camp I'm going to make sure to clear that old box, all right. How about the rest - do you say go?" asked Jerry.

"Count me in," called Will.

"Yes, you will want to get some views of the old trapper and his cabin, with the door covered with muskrat skins," remarked Frank.

"Coming along, Bluff?" asked Jerry, watching the other covertly.

"I guess not to-day. I'm going to hunt around again to see if I could have unconsciously grabbed up that gun as I bolted, and then dropped it in the brush. Such a thing might happen, you know, fellows," returned the other.

So he remained behind when the other three sallied forth, Frank and Jerry carrying their guns over their shoulders, while Will brought up the rear bearing his camera ready for use and on the lookout for subjects.

"If you see any game please give me a chance to snap a view before you shoot," he pleaded; at which the others laughed.

"Perhaps, but we can't promise. If a partridge got up suddenly it would be a case of shoot first, and think afterwards," said Frank.

"But if it should be a deer standing feeding?"

"Or a black bear on his hind legs begging?" jeered Jerry.

"All right. I'm going to be ready for all that comes along. Still life, if I have to, or anything else."

Will's last words were drowned in the report of Jerry's gun. He had swung it around like a flash, and without apparently glancing along the barrels, fired one charge at something that was flashing through the undergrowth.

There came a second shot, so close upon the heels of the first that the reports were almost blended in one.

Jerry turned and looked reproachfully at Frank.

"Talk about your sporting blood, you sure wiped my eye that time," he said.

"The bird was a little too close for your shot to scatter; I had a better chance as it flew away farther. You'd have dropped him with your second barrel, I reckon, old fellow," cried Frank, hurrying forward to pick up the partridge.

"Yes, I've no doubt I would; but that's the first time I ever had any one step in and beat me clean. I'll have to watch out for you after this, you sly 'possum. But then you've shot lots of these birds up in Maine, I suppose?"

"Plenty of them; but up there they light in trees, and the natives don't hesitate to drop them while they sit."

"That's little short of murder," said Jerry.

After an hour's walk they reached the camp of old Jesse.

"There it is, boys," said Frank, pointing ahead.

"And he's home, too; something I hardly expected at this time of day," from Jerry. "Because if he has a line of traps the morning is the time he tends them, I'm told."

As they approached, the man in the camp turned and saw them. He was a tall and angular fellow, well on in years, and with keen eyes that seemed always looking for signs around him.

"Say, boys, this here is right nice o' you, comin' to look me up. Out on a leetle hunt to-day?" he asked, as he shook hands all around.

"We've come up to camp out for a couple of weeks, while repairs are made to the school building, damaged in the gale of wind," answered Frank.

"Sho, ye don't say? Well, now, that's fine! I'll be right glad to see sumpin' o' ye while around. Whar's the camp, Jerry?"

"At the spring under the twin hemlocks. We wanted to run over and see how you were getting on. Started to put out your traps yet, Jesse?" asked the other.

"Oh! I got a few in line. Season's a bit early yet, ye see. Bringing in some musquash," and he swept his hand around at a dozen wooden frames upon which the skins were drying in the shade.

"Please let me get a picture of you at work, just as you were when we came up," said the ambitious photographer, keen on the subject that interested him most.

The trapper grinned good-naturedly.

"Fire away, then. So long as I don't give away any o' my secret ways o' preparin' the pelts, I don't keer. I'm some proud o' that shack, too. Sheds the rain, an' kin be kept warm easy; what more do a feller want?" he observed.

The operation was speedily completed.

"Hope you feel better now you've got that out of your system," said Jerry.

"I have five more exposures on this roll of film, boys. Hope to get something worth while before we start back to camp," retorted Will, caressing his new camera.

"Where do you get the muskrats, Jesse?" asked Frank, as he bent down to examine the way in which each skin was carefully stretched out on its little frame.

"Along the edge o' the swamp half a mile off. They's jest rafts o' 'em thar. As a rule the pelts bring about fifteen cents each, but jest now thar's quite a boom on, an' I reckon I'll git sixty apiece."

"That's fine. What else do you catch here in season?" asked Jerry.

"Wall, a few mink, not many, once in a long while an otter, fur which I git twenty dollars. Then I caught three bobcats last winter, seven foxes, eleven 'coon, half a dozen 'possums, an' two black b'ars, though one o' them I shot arter we had a right lively argyment."

"Whew! then there *are* bears around here?" asked Will, eagerly; "what wouldn't I give to get a picture of one in its wild state?"

The old man laughed.

"Kinder risky business a shootin' *that* thing at a b'ar, 'specially a she-b'ar as has young uns nigh. Like as not she'd rush ye. Now, I got a skin here with the head on it, an' if it comes to the wust we might rig that up, natural like, so ye cud git a picter o' a wild an' ferocious beast coming at ye on his hind legs."

"Oh! I hope I won't have to descend to a fake like that. But we've come to put in the day with you, Jesse. Show us how you set your traps, won't you?"

"Sartin I will. Was jest startin' out for a turn when ye showed up; so s'pose ye drop in line. It won't take more'n an hour or two, boys."

They were delighted at the chance, Will lugging his camera along, though the old trapper cast a dubious eye on the affair, as if he did not wholly like the idea of visiting his traps with such a "contraption," something unheard of in his experience.

"Now, don't even whisper, fellers. Here's the swamp and my traps begins clost by. I'll show ye all about it by signs. Dumb trappers is most successful, they sez," remarked Jesse, holding up his hand.

The three boys followed close at his heels, each picking his way, and walking on his tiptoes, as though that would make any difference.

So they entered the edge of the swamp.

Suddenly the man came to a halt and stooping, pointed ahead.

"Looky yonder," he whispered hoarsely, "that's somebody stealing out o' my traps!"

CHAPTER VIII

WHERE IS BLUFF?

"Where?" gasped Will, making as if anxious to get a snapshot of the thief in the very act.

"Keep quiet!" whispered Frank, giving him a push.

There was some one bending over the edge of the water, for they could catch a glimpse of his back.

"Stay here an' watch me scare the critter!" said old Jesse, with a frown.

He glided forward, very like an Indian brave creeping up on his enemy. Whoever the offender might be, he seemed to have no suspicion that danger hung over his head.

Suddenly the trapper jumped forward, and the boys saw him seize his prey.

"Wow! talk about your wildcats springing, that was a corker!"

Jerry led the way forward, though hard put to it to keep ahead of his eager companions, anxious to assist the trapper if he needed help.

"Take that, you pelt thief, and that! Let me ketch ye at my traps agin an' I'll jest waste a bullet on one o' yer legs. Kim up here an' steal my skins, will ye? Thar's another fur ye. Oh, howl all ye want to, I'm larnin' ye a lesson."

The hearty kicks with which he punctuated this speech brought forth a whoop of pain from the recipient on each occasion.

"Why, it's Pet Peters!" exclaimed Frank.

There was a snap.

"Thank you!" cried Will, with a satisfied grin; he had succeeded in taking a snapshot of the struggling couple while their faces were exposed.

"It'll do as evidence when I want ter send this critter to jail, which I'll sartin do if he ever comes a foolin' 'round my traps agin. I bet that snake Bud Rabig set him up ter it. Skeered to come hisself, an' sends a boy. Now, you git!"

This time the kick was so tremendous that it actually lifted Andy Lasher's crony clear off his feet, and started him in a mad flight along the edge of the swamp. As he ran wildly he kept bellowing in pain, and holding both hands back of him.

The temptation was more than Will could stand, and another "click" announced that he had secured a second retreating view of the poacher.

"At this rate I'll soon have my six rolls done," he announced, triumphantly.

"What harm did he do?" asked Frank.

The trapper made an investigation.

"Jest ketched him in time. Ye see he bed got the game outen the steel, an' was tryin' to sot the trap again so as I wouldn't know it. That proves he was sent up here by that sneakin' Bud

Rabig; fur what would the boy know about fixin' a trap if he didn't git guided?"

Jerry picked up the drowned muskrat and examined it.

"Pretty soft fur it has. Lots of it used nowadays I understand," he observed.

"Yas, but mostly under other names. Fur is a-gittin' skeercer all the time, an' they hev to come to stuff they used to larf at. Now watch me sot her, boys."

They were all interested in the manner in which the trap was set, for much care and ingenuity is required in order to outwit the cautious instincts of the animal; though muskrats are not half so timid as some other animals whose fur is coveted by the trappers.

"Now fur the next trap. Hope I don't find a thief has be'n thar too," said Jesse.

Evidently Pet Peters had just started in to follow up the line of traps, as described to him by Bud Rabig the rival of old Jesse, for they saw no more evidences of a visit.

When an hour had passed they were carrying five victims of the steel traps.

Jerry did not much fancy the business.

He tried to be a thorough sportsman all the time, and anything that savored of the habits of a game butcher, or trapping and shooting for the market, grated on his nerves.

After this Jesse led them to where he had a bear trap located, and here they were compelled to exercise considerable caution, because Bruin is a suspicious beast, and easily frightened away.

But the trap was not sprung; and Jesse from a little distance explained to his young friends how it lay concealed under the fallen leaves at a place where he knew a bear frequented in passing to and fro.

"I'm goin' to look up his den in a few days, before he shuts in fur the winter, an' sot my trap, whar he's jest bound to tread in it goin' or comin'. Now, if so be ye feels that way, let's git back to camp an' hatch up some sorter dinner Ever eat musquash, boys?"

"What, eat muskrats?" exclaimed Jerry, in disgust.

"I never have, but would like to try the dish," remarked Frank. "Up in Maine the trappers told me they were fine in winter weather."

Will said not a word, but his lip curled, as though nothing could tempt him to even take a taste of such a queer dish.

It was high noon when they arrived at the shack of the old trapper, and all of the boys felt sharp pressed with hunger.

"I hope he's got something else besides muskrat - ugh!" said Jerry to Will.

"I saw part of a deer hanging up before we left here," replied the other.

Jerry licked his lips in anticipation.

"Venison, real venison, fresh in the woods! Tell me about that, will you? I'm in on that deal every time. I hope he cooks enough of it."

There was little danger of the trapper allowing any of his guests to go hungry.

"Boys, I want you all to help me git a fine dinner. Frank, I knows you are used to makin' up a good cookin' fire, you 'tend to that part Jerry, see that ere haunch o' venison hangin' from the limb o' that tree - jest git her down an' cut off some slices, all this here big fry-pan'll hold, an' put some pieces o' salt pork in along with it, 'cause ye see venison is mighty dry. Bill, p'raps ye kin look arter the coffee part o' the bizness."

Immediately everybody became busy.

Old Jesse went away with a couple of the muskrats, and when he came back later he had them skinned and ready for cooking; an operation the boys watched with considerable uneasiness.

Finally the meal was ready, and they sat down.

The venison tasted prime, and the coffee was pretty good; at least it was hot, and on a cool day that counts for a good deal.

Jerry and Will watched their comrade bravely take a portion of the musquash.

"How is it?" asked Jerry, for there had not been enough of the venison after all to appease their appetites.

"Bully. Just try for yourselves. I've eaten much worse dishes right at home," was the immediate reply of the stout-hearted Frank.

Old Jesse chuckled and gave him a look of appreciation.

Thereupon both of the others took a very dainty help, and with much hesitation tasted of the dish; but both came back for more, and in the end pronounced the new dish all right.

"Why, fellows," said Frank, laughing, "it was the same with terrapin years ago. People along the Eastern Shore used to consider the diamond-back as common as dirt."

"So I was reading the other day," admitted Jerry.

"Yes, sir, so common that when men hired out they stipulated in the bond that they were not to be fed on terrapin. Then the fashionable people took a fancy for the dish, the supply ran low, and now a decent-sized terrapin is worth five dollars. Perhaps muskrats may become popular the same way, who knows?" laughed Frank.

At which the trapper roared, seemingly thinking it a great joke.

He showed them how he took the skins off, and stretched them on his frames.

"Not too tight, boys; and then keep 'em in the open air in the shade, away from the fire, till they gits right dry. Some we take off whole, an' others is slit up, jest accordin' to the kind."

All this sort of thing was eagerly listened to, especially by Frank and Jerry, always interested in everything that pertained to hunting and wild animals.

Will had his mind bent upon one subject, and could not bear to think of anything else; in camp and out, he kept his eyes on the alert for subjects suitable for striking pictures with which to embellish his account of the outing trip.

So the afternoon began to wane almost before they were aware of it.

"Time we were making tracks for home, fellows," announced Frank.

"What will Bluff and Toby think has become of us, I wonder,"' said Will.

"Him? Why, he's forgotten we're in existence. He can never get that jay gun out of his mind. Talk about your phonograph, he's sure the worst repeater I ever heard, and that's no fairy story," grunted Jerry.

"Well, come along boys. Jesse, you must run over and have dinner with us some afternoon. We dine at night, you see. Will you come?" asked Frank, shaking hands.

"I sartin will, and soon at that. Glad ye thought 'bout the ole lone trapper, boys. Come agin, soon, an' any time. An', Bill, when ye git them picters printed remember I'm in one, an' that pelt thief, too."

"I'll see you get copies of both. Good-by!" called out Will.

They trudged back with less ambition to make time than when on the morning tramp, for all of them were feeling a little stiff. As they came in sight of the home camp, Jerry broke out with:

"Say, she looks some nice, with the two tents standing there, and old Toby working around."

"Do you see Bluff?" asked Frank, a trifle uneasily.

"Why, no, but what makes you say that?"

"I've got a suspicion about him, that's all Hello, Toby, everything all right?"

"Sho, Marse Frank, eberything am lubly an' de goose hangs high."

"How about Bluff - where is he?"

"Don't no nuffin' 'bout dat boy; he went off in de mornin' an' ain't kim back."

"Just what I feared, fellows," said Frank. "That silly chap has gone hunting up the camp of the Lasher crowd, and like as not got himself in trouble."

CHAPTER IX

JERRY TAKES CHANCES

The announcement of Frank stunned both the others for a moment.

"Do you really believe that?" asked Will, uneasily, at length.

"It would be just like Bluff to take chances. He never counts the cost. Yes, sir, I just wager he started for that camp before we had been gone half an hour."

"But how would he know where to find those fellows?" asked Will.

"Oh! he knew, all right. We talked it over last night when you were busy with your camera, after we chased around for the stone-thrower; and agreed that since Andy and his mates couldn't get this camp-site, the next best place for them to go would be that little cabin up near the shore of the lake," said Jerry.

"You mean the one the charcoal burners used to live in long ago?"

"Yes. And as Bluff has been around this section more than once, he must have known how to get there. Five to one he burst right into the camp and demanded his gun."

"Do you think so?" said Jerry, uneasily.

"That is his way. And you can just guess that he got into hot water before half a minute had gone," returned Frank.

"Would they hurt Bluff?" asked Will, beginning to show unexpected feeling.

"Well, they might, especially if he accused them of stealing his gun. Besides, if he happened to see it there I wouldn't put it past Bluff to tackle the whole bunch in the effort to get his property," Frank went on.

Jerry had thrown his gun down as if ready to drop over himself. He now stooped and picked it up again.

"Come on, fellows; there's only one thing for us to do," he said.

"And that's to hike over to that shanty and find out if they've got our chum there a prisoner," finished Frank.

Will made no move to leave his beloved camera behind.

"Hide it somewhere," suggested Frank; "for it will be too dark by the time we get across to their camp to take a picture decently."

"I guess not," observed the other, calmly; "you see I'm prepared to snap off a flashlight picture at any old time. Here's after you, Frank."

Uncle Toby had witnessed this threatened exodus with signs of alarm.

"Whar ye gwine, Marse Frank? Ain't 'spectin' to leab dis chile erlone hyah be yuh? I doan't like dem owls a-whoopin' dar in de big timber: an' I sure reckons dar might be bars an' wildcats a-snoopin' round dis yer camp ter-night."

"We expect to be back before a great while, Uncle Toby. Just be getting supper ready for us in an hour or so. And have a good fire. Wild beasts will never trouble any one when backed by a blaze, remember. So-long!"

When they looked back, they could see the ancient darkey gazing with longing glances, as if he might be tempted to chase after them.

"Do you think Bluff can be in trouble?" asked Jerry, showing real solicitude in his voice and manner.

"I'm a little afraid of it. And I want to say right here that both of you have shown the right spirit in agreeing to come with me so quickly. It does you credit, boys," remarked Frank.

Will seemed to puff up a bit under the compliment, but Jerry sneered.

"Oh! I don't consider that anything at all. Bluff is a good fellow in spite of his butcher instincts, and I guess he'd go out of his way to help me," he said.

Frank looked at him, and opened his mouth to speak, but on second thought changed his mind.

Jerry seemed to know more about the woods than either of his chums. He had little trouble in guiding them across the territory that separated the rival camps, which was not more than a mile or so.

"I can see the glow of a fire ahead," announced Will, presently.

"That's the place we're aiming for; the lake lies beyond. I've fished from the point many a time," pursued Jerry.

"And when are we going to try for fish; I brought my rod and lines along, thinking we'd have a fish dinner some fine day?" complained Will.

"Wait, there's plenty of time. The season is nearly over, but if a warm day comes along we ought to be able to get some bass, I think," remarked Frank, who was something of an authority in that line.

"I can see figures moving about like black ghosts," announced Jerry. "Say, fellows, this is getting real exciting, creeping up on a rival camp with the intention of holding up the whole kit at the muzzle of our guns."

"Oh! I hope it won't come to such a desperate point as that. I'd rather not have any trouble with that Lasher if it can be avoided," ventured Frank.

"But if they've got our chum tied to a tree a prisoner?" demanded Jerry.

"In that case we'll make sure that he's set free, no matter what the consequences," was the immediate response from the leader.

As they drew nearer to the fire they could begin to make out the identity of those who were moving about.

Andy Lasher could be easily seen, as he always took it upon himself to be the high pin of any gathering of the clans in which he moved; then there was the fellow who had been caught stealing from the traps of Jesse Wilcox that morning, still limping painfully whenever he walked.

Besides these two there were five other boys present

"A tough-looking bunch," muttered Jerry, as he trailed along after Frank.

"I don't see anything of Bluff, though," whispered the other, over his shoulder.

"Perhaps they've got him inside the cabin. If you two would

agree to stay here, I'll volunteer to creep up back of it and find out," said Jerry.

"You're all right, old fellow. Just the kind to tie to," replied Frank.

"Oh! I don't know. Any one of you would do the same for me. Besides, I guess - but then, it doesn't matter. Will you wait here, boys?" asked Jerry.

"Draw a little closer. Then let Will have your gun while you're away."

Jerry handed it over a little regretfully; indeed, he had calculated on carrying the weapon himself, though it must have been in the way.

They saw him creep off.

For quite some little time they watched, ready to rush forward if any sound announced that Jerry had been discovered, and was in trouble.

"They're getting supper. Don't look like our outfit, does it?" whispered Will, as he and Frank crouched there in the brush, waiting and watching.

"I should say not; still, the appetite is the main thing in the woods. A hungry man can forgive anything. Look behind the shack - isn 't that something moving?"

What Frank had said was true, for just then Jerry crept across an open space, and for a few seconds they saw him plainly.

Then he daringly slipped in through the open door of the cabin, doubtless taking advantage of the attention of the campers being turned elsewhere.

"Come on, move up a little. I'm too nervous now to stay

quiet," said Frank.

While they were thus advancing there suddenly arose a tremendous clamor. It appeared to issue from the interior of the dilapidated cabin in which Andy's crowd had taken up their quarters.

"Oh! what has happened now?" exclaimed Will, scrambling to his feet.

"Look!" cried Frank.

Something came flying out of the door of the shack, and landing in a heap rolled over and over, clawing at every object within reach.

Then it sat up and looked around in a frightened way.

"Why, it's Ben Cooper!" said Will, partly relieved.

"And he's met up with Jerry!" added Frank, grimly, as he watched eagerly to see what else took place in the little opening where the camp had been pitched.

The boys were all on their feet. They seemed to be staring at their half-dazed comrade as though hardly able to grasp the real meaning of the conditions.

Then Andy gave a shout.

"Hey, you fellers, look at that door go shut! The prisoner must have got loose! How about it, Ben Cooper? What happened to you?"

"They's another feller in there 'sides the prisoner. He knocked me clean silly, and threw me out o' the door," whined the other, rubbing his head dismally.

"Who was it - any of that crowd from over by the hemlocks?"

demanded Andy, much excited, and apparently ready to tear up things generally.

"I reckon 'twar that Jerry Wallington - wait till I gets him some day, that's all."

"Hey, fellers, d'ye hear that? Another of that lot bagged in the cabin. Come on, an' we'll do him up!" yelled the brawny leader, rushing forward.

When he reached the door, he tried in vain to break it open. It seemed to be braced in such a manner that he could make no impression on the planks.

"Bring me the ax, somebody!" he howled, after beating his fists vainly against the panel.

One of his followers made haste to obey. When Andy was aroused in this way the bravest of them did not dare brook his anger.

He immediately swung the implement about his head.

Crash! went the ax into the door, which began to split under the vigorous assault, as though unable to stand long before such tactics.

"He'll do it - he's going to break his way in; and I've got Jerry's gun! Oh! dear what shall we do?" exclaimed Will.

"Stop that chopping, you!" shouted Frank, running forward with raised gun.

CHAPTER X

UNCLE TOBY FLIES HIGH

"Here, don't shoot!" shouted Andy, dodging behind one of his companions.

"We surrender!" cried another, throwing up his hands.

Frank and Will looked very threatening as they advanced. Both of them had their guns leveled, and besides, the latter was encumbered with his camera, so that he presented the appearance of being fairly loaded down with war material.

"Hey, Jerry, open up!" called Frank.

The door of the shack immediately began to move, and presently it was shoved aside, with the ax still sticking in its planking, just as Andy had left it.

"Talk about your rescue parties, say, don't this take the cake?" exclaimed a familiar voice, and Jerry's head was thrust out of the opening.

"Is Bluff there?" demanded Frank.

"Sure," came in the voice of their missing chum.

A second head had by this time shown up.

"Hey, you, Franky boy, what d'ye mean bombarding our camp in this way? What have we done to your crowd, I'd like to know, to be treated like dogs? First there was that Bluff Masters a-walkin' in here an' accusing us of stealing his blamed old gun, when the only one we've got is a musket Pet owns. Now you come tearing up things."

Andy was evidently getting indignant; but all the same he kept on the watch, and whenever he thought he saw one of those weapons pointing in his direction he slipped quietly behind one of the others.

"That's all right. Bluff has lost his gun; somebody took it from our camp last night just after a shower of rocks came in on us and we rushed out to find the fellow who sent them. He thought it was one of your crowd, and I guess he came over to ask. What business had you tying him up like a convict, tell me that?"

Frank put this to him sternly. At the same time he beckoned to Jerry to make a start out of the cabin, which the other easily understood, and set about obeying.

"Why, the silly fool was for trying to lick the whole lot of us; said as how he knew somebody from here had swiped his old gun, and that unless we handed it over he'd show us. Say, we couldn't stand for that, so we just sailed in and made him a prisoner. We didn't hurt him much, no more than he did us. Suppose the lot of you clear out now, and let us alone," growled Andy, growing bolder.

"Which we will be only too glad to do. We only wanted to get Bluff back."

There was a sudden brilliant flash, and a shout of alarm from the boys about the front of the charcoal burners' cabin.

"Got it all right, and I bet it's a dandy!" exclaimed Will.

He had set down Jerry's double-barreled shotgun when he saw what he considered a good chance to get a picture of the group, and touched off the little cartridge that allowed him to snatch a flashlight picture.

Two or three of Andy's fellows threw themselves flat on the ground, under the impression that some one had fired at them; still more of them were trying to hide behind each other in alarm.

"Hey, take that feller away, won't you? He's sure enough to scare anybody out of a year's growth," shouted Andy, waving his arms excitedly.

But he knew better than to try and rush forward while Frank stood guard. There seemed to be an air of determination about that individual that Andy did not fancy.

By this time Jerry and Bluff had joined their chums.

The latter did not seem any the worse for his long confinement; indeed, he was grinning as though the scare of his enemies over that flashlight had amused him.

"We're only too willing to go. I told you before that we didn't mean to have any trouble with you, if we could help it; but if you start the ball rolling look out."

"Yes," said Will, on the heels of what Frank had said, "it's a case of millions for defense, not one cent for tribute."

"Good night, fellows, and thank you for the grub you gave me?" laughed Bluff, as he waved his hand mockingly toward the group.

Jerry had recovered his gun, and, in a bunch, the four chums walked away. The others followed them menacingly for a short distance, but every time one of the two armed lads turned there was a sudden scattering. When Will whirled around and elevated his camera they fell flat to the ground as though really alarmed.

"They've turned back," announced Jerry, presently.

"Say, that was fine of you to come in there and rescue me," declared Bluff, as he caught hold of Jerry's unwilling hand, and squeezed it.

The other seemed to be unusually modest, for he pulled quickly away.

"Beat it, Bluff. You know you'd have done the same for me. I guess I owed you something for making fun of you so much. Anyhow, it was just bully, that's what. Talk about your earthquakes and cyclones, I don't think anything could beat that scare you gave them with your old flashlight stunt, Will."

"And I reckon it's going to turn out a dandy picture. I just wanted to get that crowd in some outlandish attitude, and if it proves what I think, I've done it."

"Did they hurt you, Bluff?" asked Frank.

"Oh! well, they acted better than perhaps I had any reason to expect. We mixed up some in the start, but they were too many for me."

"You mean the whole lot - well, I should guess yes. You had a sweet nerve sauntering into that camp and taking them all on. Accused them of stealing, too! Say, you don't know that they took your gun, do you?" demanded Frank.

"N - no, perhaps not," admitted Bluff, hesitatingly.

"Just surmise like, isn't it?"

"But why that shower of stones if not to get us to run out of camp, so that some one could sneak in and take a coveted article - and what more natural than that my new repeater should be the thing they wanted?" said Bluff, logically, as he believed.

"Well, until you have found some stronger evidence than that, I'd be a little slow about accusing any of that crowd, eh, Jerry?" went on Frank.

"That's right," admitted Jerry, looking back just then as if he fancied they might be followed, which, of course, was not the case.

"You didn't see any signs of the gun while there, did you?" asked Frank.

"No, I can't say I did; but then they wouldn't be likely to stick my own property under my nose, would they? I could have them arrested later on for robbery."

"All right. Suppose we let the subject rest for a while. The gun may turn up again, sooner or later. I have heard of just such queer freaks happening in camp. Now, who gets the first sight of our campfire, and old Toby cooking a glorious supper?"

"Wow! I can do justice to it all right. They gave me something to eat, but gracious, it was burned, and tasted horrible. Not one in that crowd knows the first thing about camp cookery, and they scorch everything they try," said Bluff, sighing.

"Just keep up a little while longer. There, isn't that the fire through that bunch of trees ahead?"

"After all, you saw it yourself first, Frank. That's the fire all right. Straight this way, boys, and we'll be there in a jiffy," said Will.

They hurried on.

"I'm looking to see good old Toby; but somehow don't seem

able to clap my eyes on his honest, black face," declared Bluff.

"That's a fact, where is he? The fire is burning decently, and from that I judge he's around somewhere," remarked Frank.

"Well," broke in Will, "you know he acted as though afraid when we were starting out. Said something about the big owls in the timber getting on his nerves."

"And the varmints prowling around, waiting for a chance to eat him up. I believe the coon is hiding in one of the tents, afraid to show himself. How about that, Frank, is he such a coward" demanded Jerry.

The other laughed.

"Don't ask me," he replied, shaking his head; "it isn't quite fair to give poor old Uncle Toby away like that But we're getting close to the camp now, and, if he is around, I'll soon raise him like I did before."

"If he's let that supper burn, something is going to happen to a respectable colored gentleman I know," threatened Bluff.

"Listen to him. Talk about your fighters, this Bluff takes the cake. Why, not satisfied with trying to whip the entire Lasher crowd in a bunch, now he wants to take on poor harmless old Uncle Toby Washington Low. Perhaps after all, it's just as well such a blood-thirsty character has been robbed of his little pump-gun. Why, he'd have cleaned out the whole woods community, given half a chance," jeered Jerry.

"Come now, let that drop. I'm only joking, and you know it. I wouldn't lay a single finger on old Toby's white wool for worlds. But where is he, Frank?" said Bluff.

"Say, there's something in our camp, boys!" ejaculated Will, at that moment.

"What's that?" asked Frank, his interest suddenly aroused.

"Well, I saw something moving there - look now, there it is again, over just beside the nearer tent," whispered Will, in an awe-struck voice.

They all saw it now.

"Keeps moving all the time. Boys, it strikes me that it must be an animal of some sort!" came from the experienced Frank.

"Goodness gracious! I hope it hasn't devoured poor old Toby," gasped Will.

"Well, make your mind up on that score, for it hasn't - *yet*! Just look aloft a bit - right above where the thing is jumping about as if worrying something. What do you see astraddle that limb, eh?" asked Frank, triumphantly.

"Talk about your treed coons, why that's old Toby sitting up there, and hanging on for dear life."

"And that object in the camp is, I believe, a wildcat, worrying over our fine ham," remarked Frank, quietly raising the hammers of his shotgun.

CHAPTER XI

A NIGHT ALARM

"Oh! please don't shoot just yet; I'm nearly ready," exclaimed Will, who had been fumbling with trembling fingers at his camera while they were creeping closer.

"What do you want to do - shoot the cat with your machine?" whispered Frank, the most accommodating fellow in the world.

"Yes, that's it. Don't you see, it would be the prize of the whole bunch? Can't you let me give a flash, and shoot afterwards?" begged the ardent photographer.

Frank could not refuse.

"It would be a dandy all right, with old Toby hanging there; but look sharp, for the cat hears us whispering, and is ready to get out."

Hardly had he spoken before there came a brilliant flash.

"Got him!" shrieked the excited Will.

Then came a heavy report close to his ears, as Frank fired.

The flash had dazzled all but Frank, who managed to keep his eyes away from it. He was thus enabled to catch sight of the startled wildcat bounding for the shelter of the trees, having deserted its meal in sudden fright.

As soon as he had fired, Frank threw his gun around so as to cover the spot he expected the animal to occupy if by any chance it escaped the full effect of his first charge.

But it jumped the other way, and might have vanished from view only that Jerry fired from his hip, there being no time to aim from the shoulder.

"He's down!" shouted Bluff, as the fierce visitor in the camp rolled over and over, clawing aimlessly as it expired.

Ready to shoot again if necessary, the two hunters cautiously advanced. There was no need of further attention, for the wildcat stiffened out under their eyes.

"Ginger! but ain't he a beaut?" exclaimed Bluff, bending over.

"I wonder if there happens to be a mate around?" said Jerry, as he bent an anxious look toward the timber close at hand.

"They generally hunt in couples," admitted Frank; "but in this case I hardly think it can be so, for the other would have come to the feast."

Uncle Toby came down from his perch rather dubiously, as if he feared that the danger might not be all over.

"What happened to you, Uncle Toby?" asked Frank, giving the others a wink not to joke the old fellow too seriously, for he was still trembling.

"Yuh see 'twar dis way, Marse Frank: dat cat he jest wanted de ham more'n Unc Toby did, an' I naturally lets him hab it. He jumps down from de tree, an' I feels a notion to elevate 'bout dat time. Don' know how I gits up dar, but 'spect I done fly," explained the cook, as well as his chattering teeth would permit.

"He means he aviated upward," grinned Jerry.

Will was patting his camera lovingly.

"Oh! I do hope it turns out fine," he said; "for that would be a jolly hit. I'd rather snap off pictures like that than shoot a grizzly or a bull moose. Me for the gentle life. I'm no butcher."

"Talk to me about that, will you? You're a sport all right, Will, only it happens that your tastes run in a different direction from mine. Don't knock my love of fair play, and I won't laugh at your wanting to snap off every living thing you see, to make up a freak collection."

"All right, then, Jerry; consider it a bargain. I suppose you'll have a muff made out of this nice fur for somebody?" continued Will, stroking the cat.

"Haven't given it a thought. Besides, half of the honor belongs to Frank."

"What's that? I made a mess of it, and the beast would have escaped if you hadn't shot him on the jump?" exclaimed Frank.

"And if you hadn't wounded him how could I have ever had a chance to shoot? You can't get out of it, old man; we'll share the honors," returned Jerry.

Frank said no more, but such generosity only drew him closer to his chum.

Fortunately the supper had not advanced far enough to be ruined. They were able to save most of the ham, which was a comfort. Frank declared that he wondered at the beast taking to smoked pork; he could not remember any similar circumstance in all his hunting, and concluded that possibly the wildcat must have been unusually hungry.

It had really been quite a strenuous day, and the boys were glad to sit around the big fire and partake of the good supper which Uncle Toby prepared.

Bluff had to relate his story again and again, but it differed little from what he had already told.

"I made a silly fool of myself, I know now, and it was mighty fine in you fellows coming to pull me out of the hole I dropped into. If that Andy has got my beautiful gun in his camp, he's smart enough to keep it under cover. I never had even a peep at it. But just wait. I'm going to get that gun back if it takes all winter," declared Bluff.

"He'll do it too, just mark me," observed Frank, nodding to Jerry.

Apparently the other was tired of hearing about that same gun, for he only smiled and shrugged his shoulders.

In the morning Jerry tried his hand at skinning the game. He had taken particular pains to notice just how old Jesse Wilcox did this sort of thing, and, being a clever imitator, he managed to succeed after a fashion.

Frank meanwhile had made a frame suitable to the size of the skin, and upon this the hairy pelt was stretched, care being taken to keep it in the shade, and not near the heat of the fire, while drying.

Later on in the day Jerry and Frank took a stroll through the woods, and managed to bring back three partridge and several gray squirrels. Frank would not let Toby cook the latter as the other wished.

"They are always tough for frying unless parboiled first. After skinning and cutting up I always put the pieces in a pot, and boil until tender; then take them out, dry off, and put them in a hot pan in which several pieces of salt pork have been first tried out. I think you'll say they're all right when you get your teeth in them, fellows," he remarked.

And they did.

Will managed to take a few views during the middle of the day, prowling in the neighborhood of the camp. There was a pretty stream not far away, and it ran over rocks and between attractive banks, so that half a dozen charming pictures presented themselves to the eyes of the artist.

The Fall had not advanced so far as to show signs of ice on the water, though there were times when the air was very crisp and frosty.

Bluff had remained in camp pretty much all day. He seemed uneasy, and passed in and out of the tents frequently as though wondering what could have happened to bring about such a mysterious disappearance of his beloved gun.

Sitting by the fire for a time, he would conceive some idea, and jumping to his feet hurry into the woods to search a particular spot where he remembered having passed over on that never-to-be-forgotten night.

Still, when the others returned in the afternoon there was the same look of distress upon his face.

"Talk to me about a pagan and his idols," said Jerry, aside to Frank; "Bluff has the whole show beaten. I never saw such a persistent fellow, never."

"He'll never be happy till he gets it, Jerry," remarked the other.

"Then he deserves to have a bad time," declared Jerry, tossing the bunch of game down before Will and Uncle Toby, who happened to be doing something in common at the campfire.

That night they had a royal feast indeed. It tasted all the better because the squirrels and partridge had fallen to their own guns, and not been basely purchased in the market. And doubtless their surroundings had considerable to do with the enjoyment of the dinner.

Will took advantage of the darkness to get a new roll of films in his camera.

"How many have you cracked off," asked Jerry, noting his occupation.

"Three rolls, so far; about half I brought. I expect to be careful from now on, and try to get choice subjects. But I know I'll never find another to equal that wildcat scene. Oh! I hope it is a success!" replied the enthusiastic photographer.

"So say we all," remarked Frank; "for it will chase the blues away many a time, just to see the look on Uncle Toby's face, as he clung to that friendly limb."

"Gorry, but I was mighty glad tuh git my claws on dat limb, Marse Frank. Wen I seed dem big yaller eyes a-starin' at me, an' heerd dat yowlin' noise, my knees dey jest wobbled together. Nevah could tell how I got up dar; reckons as how you say am jest de truf, an' I *flew*!" exclaimed the cook, able to laugh now at his adventure.

They turned in early, for their rest had been broken on the preceding night, and both the hunters were leg weary.

The last sound Frank remembered hearing was the mournful hooting of the owls. The birds seemed to have a favorite roosting-place not far away, and from time to time the tremulous sound of their calling drifted through space.

Just how long he slept Frank did not exactly know. He awoke with a sneeze, and sat up, rubbing his eyes.

"What's the matter?" exclaimed Jerry, also starting out of a sound sleep.

"I don't know - why, the tent's full of smoke! The camp must be on fire! Wake up, everybody!"

As the two lads came crawling out of the canvas they were startled to discover a heavy pall of smoke rising all around them.

CHAPTER XII

THE TELL-TALE MATCH-SAFE

"Wake up! wake up!"

Both Frank and Jerry shouted at the top of their strong voices. The others came tumbling into view, and loud were their expressions of dismay at the terrible sight that met their eyes.

"Get busy here, every one! Water wanted, and never mind your clothes!"

Even while he was speaking Frank jumped into action. The night air struck home, and made him shiver, for he had just tumbled out from between the snug folds of his blanket; but this was a time when delay might mean the complete wiping out of the camp.

Will gave a whoop and immediately vanished again inside the tent. He had not gone to rescue any of his clothes, nor did he even think of getting into them; but when he reappeared it was with his camera hugged tightly in his arms.

Meanwhile the others had set to work with a vim. There was fortunately no wind, so that the fire had burned sluggishly. Then again the late storm had wet the dead leaves then on the ground, and they had not as yet become thoroughly dry, so it took quite some time for them to get over smouldering, and burst into a vigorous flame.

"We're getting it down, fellows; keep right along hitting it hard!" called Frank, cheerily.

Even old Toby had appeared from under the fly where he slept. He had been dreadfully scared at first, doubtless under the impression that the mate to the dead bob-cat had invaded the camp, intent on revenge. This feeling soon gave way to the desire to see the camp saved, and he labored faithfully with the rest.

Scattering the smouldering leaves, beating out the fire with any sort of thing they could snatch up in their excitement, they managed to get the flames under control after a little while.

It had been a most exciting experience, however. Bluff was swinging his blanket vigorously, and thrashing the fire with it effectively; though he might later on have some difficulty in getting rid of the smudges that this process necessarily produced.

"Victory!" shouted Jerry, when the last vestige of the fire had gone under.

Bluff threw his blanket around his shoulders and strutted about with the air of a conqueror;

"They have to get up early in the morning if they expect to beat us," he said, proudly.

"Talk about your hot times, that was a scorcher!" cried Jerry.

"But I'm beginning to shiver now all right; and I advise every one to crawl into his clothes in a hurry. Then we can talk it over. It's a mighty suspicious thing, that's what," remarked Frank.

They were only too glad to take his advice, and shortly after the four gathered around the revived campfire to exchange opinions.

They were a pretty smutty-looking crowd; but Jerry declared that those marks were medals of honor.

"Now, if we had all been like Will here, and each rushed for his possessions, the camp would have been a-goner," he remarked, with a reproachful look.

"That's all right, fellows, and under any other conditions I would have been one of the first to assist; but I'm the official photographer of the expedition, and the guardian of those splendid films that must perpetuate our camping trip, for posterity," he explained.

"Hear! hear!" cried Frank.

"Why didn't you lay the outfit down at a safe distance then, and help fight the fire with us?" demanded Bluff.

"I guess I know enough to take warning from your sad experience. They hooked your old gun; the next thing they'll be after will be my camera. No, sir, I hang on to that business through thick and thin. They'll have to chloroform me to get my films away, and that's so."

"Was it an accident?" asked Bluff, looking to Frank for an opinion.

"What do you think, Jerry?" demanded the leader.

"It couldn't have been an accident, and I'm dead sure of it," was the reply.

"Suppose you state your reasons then."

"First, we banked the fire down as usual before crawling into bed. Then there wasn't a particle of wind to scatter the sparks. And last, but not least, those heaps of dead leaves were carried here! I happen to know that place was just about bare last evening!" replied the other, seriously.

Will uttered an exclamation of wonder and alarm.

"Do you really mean to say that some fellows would be mean enough to try and burn our camp?" he asked.

"I wouldn't put it past that Andy Lasher. Talk to me about your heathen! he's just about equal to any of 'em. But don't you agree with me, Frank?"

"Certainly I do, because I happen to have a strong bit of evidence which I picked up out there close to the burning leaves."

He held something up.

"A match-box!" exclaimed Will.

"Do any of you own that?"

"Pass it around. I never saw it before," declared Jerry, as he handled the little silver article in which several matches still remained.

"Well, I have, then," remarked Bluff, suddenly, as he stared at the trophy; "and just as I thought, here are two initials on it."

"What are they?" asked Jerry, showing excitement.

"H.B."

"That doesn't cover any of Andy's crowd, though," said Jerry, seemingly disappointed.

"The real owner of this match-box is Herman Bancroft," announced Bluff; "I've had it in my hands more than once. You know I went with him for a time."

"He wanted to join our Rod, Gun and Camera Club, but the black ball dished his chances. Perhaps Herman was mad about that; perhaps he even followed us up here, and has tried to get even," suggested Will.

"That's hard to believe, for he isn't the bad fellow some people say. A little wild, but with a good heart. I'd rather believe he lost it, and one of that crowd picked it up," said Bluff, sturdily.

"That's just like you, Bluff, standing up for a friend. Well, I'm rather inclined to believe the same way. Anyhow, it was a mighty mean dodge. If that Andy Lasher keeps on he'll get in a peck of trouble sooner or later. Why, for such a thing as this he deserves a peppering of shot at a distance," said Frank, indignantly.

"It was criminal, that's what. We might have been smothered in our beds," remarked Bluff.

"Or my camera might have been utterly destroyed," wailed Will.

Old Toby said nothing, but he cast many an anxious look around at the adjacent trees, as if he had an idea lingering under his woolly pate thatin some way or other this new disaster might have a connection with the shooting of the wildcat.

Things assumed a normal aspect after a while, and only for the scent of burnt leaves no one would dream that the camp had come near destruction.

But all the inmates of Kamp Kill Kare slept, so to speak, "with one eye open" during the balance of that night.

There was no further alarm.

By the time breakfast had been disposed of they could look the matter calmly in the face, and it no longer appeared in such a terrible aspect as when they were scampering around in their pajamas fighting the flames and smoke.

The sun seemed unusually warm this morning, so Will declared that he meant to tramp over to the lake and try a little fishing, since they would have small opportunity to do any of this when the cold winds came again.

"I'm on too," remarked Bluff, moodily; "a fellow without a gun is like a fifth wheel to a wagon, useless in camp. Let's make up some lunch, for it's a long tramp, and we won't come home until late."

Jerry announced that he wanted to go over and have a further talk with Jesse Wilcox; after which he might take a tramp in a new region advised by the old trapper as opening a possible chance for big game - perhaps a deer.

Frank declared he would stick to the camp; with such vicious characters around, he secretly thought it hardly safe for all of them to go away, leaving old Toby as the sole guardian. They had too much at stake, since their pleasure would be destroyed if the camp were raided successfully.

Reaching the lake Will spent much of his time taking views, while Bluff set to work trying to entice the finny denizens of the water to bite his lures.

As time went on he was fairly successful, and when they ate their lunch he had quite a fair string of fish as the reward of his diligence.

Will proved to be a poor fisherman after all, especially when he had his adored camera along, for he presently wandered off again.

"Don't go too far," warned Bluff, as he sat on the end of a log that jutted out over the water a yard or more.

Engrossed with his sport, Bluff hardly noticed how time passed. Hearing a step back of him, he called out:

"I got three more; what luck did you have, Will?"

He heard what sounded like a chuckling laugh back of him; and before he could turn some one gave him a strong push. Bluff went over with a splash into the lake.

CHAPTER XIII

THE COMING OF THE STORM

Bluff came up spluttering.

"Help! help!" he shouted, involuntarily, as well as a mouth half full of water would permit.

But there was no one in sight. Whoever had shoved him into the lake had mysteriously vanished, though a movement in the bushes told the direction of his flight.

Recovering from the shock, Bluff found that he could clamber out without much difficulty, and he hastened to do so.

His cries had been heard, however, for presently the sound of some one running wildly came to his ears, and Will burst into view.

At sight of the dripping fisherman he broke into a shout.

"Caught a Tartar, did you, and he pulled you in? Oh! what wouldn't I have just given to have been here? A snapshot of you going over would have been the finest ever."

"Shut up! It wasn't a fish at all that yanked me overboard. Somebody gave me a shove!" snapped Bluff, beginning to shiver, in spite of the fact that the air seemed unusually warm, though the sun had disappeared behind dark clouds.

"What! you were pushed in?" stammered Will; and he gathered up his camera in his arms, casting a look of alarm around, as if afraid lest some hideous form dart into view, bent on snatching it away.

"That's the truth. I was just sitting here when I heard a step. Thought it was you, and asked how you had got on. Then the beggar laughed, gave me a shove, and over I went, 'ker chunk.' I let out a yell when I came up, for you see I didn't exactly know what he might mean to do," explained the dripping one.

"And I don't blame you a bit. But didn't you see him at all?"

"Never had a peep. He dodged back so that when I got the water out of my eyes he was gone. I saw those bushes over there moving, and knew he ran off that way."

Will walked over to the bushes, looking cautiously about, but seeing no one.

"Sure you didn't - er - go to sleep out on that log, and dream somebody gave you a push?" he queried, cautiously.

"Rats! I guess I ought to know. But see here, perhaps you can prove it," declared Bluff, indignantly.

"How?" demanded the other.

"Look down at your feet and see if he left any trail, that's how."

Will immediately did as he was told.

"Say, come here. There are tracks all right. Perhaps you're better up in that sort of thing than I am. It was a human being after all, and no dream," he called.

Bluff hastened to join him.

"Why, of course, just as I said. This is where he hurried away. You can see the mark of his feet easy. And looky there, one shoe, the right, has got a patch on it, a piece that runs to a point. Oh! I'd know that skunk any time from that. It's a sure clue, I tell you," he exclaimed.

"But you'd better get dried off as soon as you can. Why, you're shivering now."

"Got any matches; mine are all soaked?" said Bluff, his teeth rattling together.

"I always carry a few. Yes, here they are. Let me make a quick fire, while you jump around to warm up; and Bluff, *please* keep your eye on my camera, won't you?"

"Sure," replied the other, commencing to leap and frisk around, so as to get his chilled blood in circulation again.

The fire was speedily made, and, taking off his clothes, Bluff hugged close to the blaze while Will busied himself in hanging up the wet garments, though he had more or less difficulty in tearing his eyes away from the spot where his camera lay close by.

"Sometimes we get too much fire; then again we want more and more," remarked Bluff, as he kept turning around like a roast on the spit; for as fast as one side felt warm the other grew chilled.

"And I guess that we'd better be beating it back to camp as soon as your duds are decently dry. I don't like the looks of that sky," remarked Will.

"I think you are right. There's certainly a big storm coming. Why, the air seems dead, just like it is in summer before a gale of wind. And camp is nearly two miles away from this place. Don't you think I could put them on now, Will?"

"They feel pretty dry. Do as you please," said the other, not willing to commit himself, though anxious to be off, for the black looks of the heavens began to appall him not a little.

"Then here goes!"

Suiting the action to the words Bluff hurriedly dressed. Then he secured his nice string of fish, and, with his pole over his shoulder, announced himself ready for the homeward tramp.

They made all reasonable haste, and managed to reach the camp in due time.

When Frank heard what had happened he was very angry.

"Some more of the mean work of that crowd. I believe it must have been Andy himself who pushed you in. A dirty trick. How did he know whether you could swim or not?" he said, after the tale was told.

"Oh, well, it wasn't a case of swimming, for the water wasn't five feet deep, and all I had to do was to crawl out again. But it was wet, you see, and a fellow feels mighty uncomfortable all soaked. Just wait, I'll get even with him some day for that trick. I've got the rascal located all right. One of his shoes had a patch on the sole I'd know again."

"A clever idea," admitted the other, in admiration; "and I hope you find him out, no matter who he may be. First they stone our camp; after that they try to burn us out; and now some busybody throws you into the lake. What next, I wonder?"

"You forget the worst thing of all - the stealing of my gun!" grumbled Bluff.

"Well, I wish Jerry was back. I hate to think of him wandering around in the woods in the storm that's coming, for it's going to be a corker," remarked Frank, eying the darkening sky with uneasiness.

"Perhaps the old trapper influenced him to stay over with him till to-morrow?" suggested Will, who was making his beloved camera secure against rain by wrapping it in folds of waterproof material brought along for the purpose.

"A bright idea; and I hope it's so. But you know, he said he meant to take in a new locality for a hunt after seeing Jesse. Well, Jerry is up to many things connected with woods life, and at any rate he knows how to look out for himself," and as he spoke Frank stooped down by the tent.

"What are you doing now?" asked the curious Bluff.

"Driving these tent pegs in deeper. There's no telling what sort of wind may be on us. Listen to that, will you?" said Frank.

"Thunder, as sure as you live! Pretty late in the year for that, ain't it?"

"Oh, we sometimes hear it even in winter. But, you see, the day has been unusually close and muggy. I felt a storm in the air this morning, and I'm not surprised. But I would be glad to see Jerry show up," continued the other, as he tapped each pin a few times, to send them in more securely.

The muttering in the distance increased constantly in volume.

Frank, as an old campaigner, knew what was to be done. Under his directions Toby and the two boys made everything as snug as could be expected. They also concealed some dry wood in the hollow of a tree nearby, so that later on they might be prepared for making a fire.

The storm came at last, with a furious wind, and a heavy downpour of rain.

"Wow!" exclaimed Bluff, as he looked out from the tent, "ain't I glad we got here before that came. One ducking satisfies me; I'm not greedy."

The afternoon waned, and night came on, still there were no signs of Jerry. Frank worried some, but stopped speaking of the matter, for he saw that old Toby was beginning to shake with fear, as the wind increased in fury, and the tents wobbled about at a great rate.

"I hope they hold out," said Frank to himself.

He even donned a waterproof he had brought along, and going outside, tapped the pegs all around again. Everything seemed secure so far as he could see. Still, he knew that if one peg gave, the balance could not resist the additional strain, and a catastrophe must result.

Old Toby was really too much alarmed to retire to his fly; so Frank told him he could remain with him when the other boys went to their tent.

None of them expected to obtain much sleep. The wind came in fierce gusts, the trees groaned and writhed, and once or twice Frank really heard a crash in the forest that told of a rent in the timber.

"I only hope nothing of that kind happens around here; a falling tree might pin us all under, and be our death," he said to himself.

At length they concluded that it was time to separate and try to get some sleep, though both Bluff and Will declared they knew they would not close their eyes so long as that howl kept up without, and the canvas fluttered with each wild gust.

Just as they were about to make a run for it, Frank caught them by the arms.

"Wait!" he shouted, for there was a terrible crash close by, and the earth seemed to tremble as a forest monarch was laid low.

At the same minute with a shriek the wind descended upon

the tent under which they were crouching.

Frank heard a snap above the other sounds, and like a flash the entire tent was blown away, leaving the four campers exposed to the fury of the storm.

CHAPTER XIV

HOW JERRY WAS TREED

Jerry, that same morning, reached the camp of the old trapper without any trouble.

He did not find Jesse Wilcox at home; but, knowing something of the trapper's habits, he made himself comfortable, and waited.

After a time the other showed up. He carried a tidy bunch of fur along with him, having stopped to remove the pelts on the way.

"Glad to see ye, Jerry. Looky here, one fine fox, and, would ye believe it, actually a mink, boy! That ere pelt orter bring me a twenty, all right. That's why I'm so tickled, ye see. This shore must be one o' my lucky days. Make yerself to hum. Come to take a snack o' dinner along with me, I reckons, eh?"

"Well, I might wait up and have a bite if you don't keep me too long. You see I mean to make a roundabout trip into that stretch of woods you told us about I'd like the worst kind to get a crack at a deer. That would be worth while, Jesse."

"Then I'll get busy right away. But p'raps ye'd better defer that ere trip fur a day or so, lad," remarked the trapper, sweeping an eye upward.

"Why?" asked the boy.

"Thar's some sorter storm broodin', er I'm bad deceived. In course at this season we don't expect much along that line; but I hev seen a scorcher come along, even in October. Ten year ago it was, and thar was quite some timber leveled, I'm tellin' ye."

But Jerry was built along a stubborn line: Having once made up his mind to do a thing it was very hard for him to break away.

"Oh! I don't bother about a little blow. If it comes to the worst I can find a hollow tree, and keep pretty dry. Now, I want to see just how you cook that stew, so I can do it sometime."

The dinner was a success, and, of course, Jerry, being hungry, heartily enjoyed it. When the meal was finished he arose, and picked up his gun.

"Still of a mind to take that long tramp, air ye?" asked the trapper.

"Why, certainly. I haven't even thought of changing my mind," returned the boy.

"Well, I s'pose ye must, then. Only keep yer eye peeled for trouble up yonder. It's sure goin' to storm; for I feels it in my bones. Besides, thar's a pack o' measly wild dogs loose in that stretch o' timber."

"Wild dogs?" repeated Jerry, opening his eyes wider.

"Sartin; dogs as has strayed away from ther homes, an' took back to a wild state. It happens that ways sometimes. Ther call o' the wild, they name it. Sumpin' seems to pull the critters back, an' they break away from human kind to roam the woods an' hunt ther livin'. I seen the pack once or twice, an' I kinder believe ther a-gettin' more fiercer all the while."

"Wild dogs, eh? How many about are there, Jesse?" asked Jerry, fingering his shotgun a little nervously.

"From three to five ginerally. Ye see they comes an' goes, so ther ain't no tellin' jest how big the pack kin be. But ef so be they tackles ye, son, jest shin up a tree, an' then pick 'em off. That's my ijee," remarked the trapper.

Shaking hands, after getting further directions, Jerry hastened away.

It was not long before he found himself in the densest kind of timber. In fact, he had not seen anything like it since coming to the hemlock camp.

Here and there were little openings, in some of which green grass grew. It was here the trapper had told him he might possibly find a deer feeding; and as he made his way along, Jerry kept on the lookout for signs.

He had been walking much over an hour when he thought he caught a glimpse of a deer ahead; there was something moving there, at least, and with his pulses quickened the boy began to slowly and cautiously advance.

Yes, it was a deer, and feeding, too!

The light was none too good under the trees, with that dark threatening sky over all; but Jerry had keen eyes and he was just now excited at the prospect of at least getting a shot.

He kept on advancing, taking advantage of every bit of cover that offered. To his delight the animal did not seem to pay any attention to him, though raising its head several times to sniff the air suspiciously.

By this time, he had gained a position where he believed he could make the buckshot in his gun tell, and with as steady a hand as he could bring to bear, Jerry took aim at the exposed side of the deer.

When he fired the animal fell in its tracks, and, giving a shout, the exultant young hunter was about rushing forward to secure his quarry when suddenly his horrified eyes discovered moving figures rushing through the undergrowth, and heading toward the spot where the deer lay, still struggling feebly.

Instantly he remembered what the trapper had said. These then were the wild dogs. Evidently they were hungry, and at the time he shot had been trying to creep up on the animal which they yearned to make a meal from.

Jerry mechanically threw out the empty shell, and pushed another into the chamber of his gun. He saw the pack bolt forward, heard the wild clamor that marked their advance, and then caught the exultant strain in their noisy yelpings, as they pounced upon the slain deer.

The boy felt more indignant than alarmed. That was *his* deer, for he had done the stalking up against the wind; nor was he at all disposed to allow those greedy curs a chance to tear the quarry to pieces in their savage way.

Jerry immediately hurried forward, ready to dispute the possession of the game.

He found the whole pack furiously tearing at the fallen deer, growling, and exhibiting all the savage nature of wolves.

When the boy shouted they looked up, drew back their lips and looked furious; but not one gave a sign of obeying him.

"Get out, you brutes! Leave that carcass alone, will you?" he yelled, waving his gun threateningly.

As if they realized that this human creature meant to dispute their right to the royal dinner they had found, the four wild dogs started toward him. They presented a terrible appearance just then, with the blood about their muzzles, and white fangs exposed.

Perhaps Jerry may have felt a shiver pass over him, but that did not prevent him from raising his gun and deliberately covering the foremost of the brutes.

Bang! went the gun. Then arose a tremendous howling, together with furious snapping sounds. The balance of the pack continued to rush forward more rapidly than before, leaving the stricken member to roll on the ground.

Jerry thought it high time he made an ascension, after the manner of that which had marked the alarm of old Toby at the time the wildcat invaded the camp. But he wanted to use that other barrel the worst way.

Quickly covering the pack he pulled the trigger. Then, without waiting to ascertain what the results might be, he started to climb.

This was no easy task, especially when encumbered with a gun, for he would not think of letting this precious ally go; but there was enough inspiration in the approaching yelps and growls of the wild dogs to spur him on to heroic efforts, and, as a consequence, he managed to get beyond their reach.

It was an old tree in which he happened to have sought refuge. Just then, however, Jerry was not caring about that, for it was a case of any port in a storm; and as he said, "beggars should not be choosers."

Quite out of breath, he clung to the rotten limb and proceeded to shout at the dogs so as to keep them there until he could find a chance to insert fresh charges in his gun, when he expected to take care of them.

"Hey, you with the collar, ain't you ashamed of yourself to take to such a pirate life, when you once had a good home, I bet? Say, ain't he a jim-dandy of a big bouncer, though, and as strong as an ox? I'd just hate to fall into his maw. Now, hang around a few seconds more, and I've got a nice surprise for you. If you ever knew what a gun is, I guess you've forgotten by now."

In this strain he talked to them, and kept both dogs jumping up at him in the endeavor to get a grip. Sometimes they brushed his dangling foot with their jaws, and at that Jerry involuntarily drew up a little.

When he had inserted the shells, he tried to get a chance to cover the big dog. That animal, though, apparently suspected his purpose, and kept jumping about so wildly that it seemed impossible to aim at him. The second brute had been wounded so seriously that it had crawled away, so there were now but two left.

Finally, seeing a good chance to knock over the smaller one of the pair, Jerry could not resist the temptation.

The animal may once have been a family pet, but a wild existence of some months, perhaps years, had taken him back to the wild state from which his ancestors had come ages ago. He was a mangy-looking, dirty white brute, with eyes that seemed red to the boy in the tree.

At the report of the gun the animal fell over in a kicking heap, for the distance was so very short that the charge of shot had gone with all the destructive power of a "forty-four" bullet.

But something not down on the programme immediately followed. The rotten limb upon which Jerry was hanging, unable to stand the strain of his weight and movements, gave way with a crash.

He felt a thrill of horror as he found himself being precipitated downward, knowing as he did that the largest and fiercest of the wild pack was still there, unhurt save in the way of a few

stray shot that had flecked his tawny hide with tiny blood spots!

CHAPTER XV

IN A BEAR'S HOLLOW

Jerry landed with a crash that almost shook the breath from his body.

Realizing the need of haste in getting upon his feet, he scrambled erect. He had maintained that frenzied clutch upon his gun, as if believing that it was his best and only friend in this emergency.

One thing helped him. The big yellow hound had been startled, first by the crash of the gun so close to his head, and then again by the rapid downward plunge of the human figure.

Perhaps some dim recollection of former beatings at the hands of some severe master may also have temporarily demoralized the brute.

At any rate Jerry was given just about five seconds to turn the corner, and thus place the tree between himself and his enemy.

Then the dog bounded forward, and a warm chase began around that same tree, with Jerry doing his prettiest to keep beyond reach of those gleaming fangs that pressed closely in his rear.

In this he managed fairly well, but after he had pranced around that tree quite a dozen times he made the alarming discovery that he was rapidly being winded. His canine adversary, on the other hand, appeared to be as fresh as ever.

Unless something occurred to assist him, it began to look very much as though he might trip after growing dizzy, and the big yellow brute pounce upon him.

Then a sudden thought came into his mind. It was like an inspiration, and made Jerry laugh right out. Why, of course his gun, what was he gripping it all this time so desperately for if not because he believed it worth while.

He tried to remember whether he had fired one shot or two after reloading it. So confused had he become with all this turning round and round that he could not be absolutely sure. But there was nothing for him to do but take chances.

He felt to see if one of the hammers might be up, and found the left one drawn back. That seemed promising, for if he had fired both barrels the hammers must naturally be down.

It might be only imagination, but he believed he could actually feel the hot breath of the pursuing beast on his legs as he twisted around that tree so awkwardly. With a prayer in his heart, though his lips were mute, he suddenly whirled, thrust out the gun, and pulled the trigger.

Fortune was certainly with him that day. The dog viciously seized hold of the gun barrel in his teeth; and it was just at this instant that Jerry pressed the trigger.

He saw the big beast swirl half-way around. Then he fell in a quivering heap.

"Hurrah!"

It was but a pitiful shout poor Jerry gave, for he was quite out of breath. He, too, fell down in a heap close to the yellow form of his enemy; but instinctively his hands worked, trying to place his faithful gun in readiness for further work.

It was not needed.

Besides the big yellow leader of the wild pack, he presently found a second brute stone dead; and had the pleasure of dispatching both the others shortly after.

"Might as well make a clean sweep of it," he said, with a feeling of having accomplished something worth while; for Jesse had told him these roving dogs were just as destructive to sheep and other domestic animals as so many timber wolves would have been.

Perhaps the farmers of the community might feel like voting Jerry thanks for his good service of that day. And not knowing whether he could find the place again he proceeded to cut off the four caudal appendages, "to embellish his tale," as Frank later on declared with a laugh.

"Guess I've had quite enough sport for to-day," Jerry remarked, as he bent over the mutilated deer; "there's quite as much meat here as I can carry home. In fact, I've a good mind to hang most of it up out of reach of wild animals. We could come for it another time. From the looks of the sky that storm Jesse spoke about must be coming right along."

So he determined to make haste. While something of a novice at the art of cutting up a deer, he had a general inkling as to how it should be done. Accordingly, after half an hour's work he managed to swing the better part of the meat, fastened up in the skin, to a limb that he made sure was sound.

"Now for home with my trophies. Say, perhaps the boys won't open their eyes when I show these four tails, and get Toby to cook some of *my* venison! This has been a red letter day in my calendar. What was that - thunder, I do believe. Perhaps - "

Jerry did not even wait to finish his sentence, but started off on a lope.

But the gloom under the heavy timber increased. He found difficulty in telling the points of the compass. And finally it became absolutely impossible for him to make more than a half-way decent guess as to the quarter where the camp in all probability lay.

"I suppose I'm just about lost," he at length reluctantly admitted.

Still, Jerry was not one to be easily daunted. He had been in situations before now that called for a show of manliness and courage, and rather prided himself on being equal to any such occasion.

The thunder was booming heavily, and the rain ready to descend. He believed he could hear a distant roaring. It might be wind tearing through the forest, or a heavy fall of rain, perhaps both. At any rate it would mark the breaking of the storm.

"Better be finding that hollow tree I spoke to Jesse about," he concluded.

Once again luck favored the lad. Not thirty paces away he discovered what seemed to be a big stump, about twelve feet or more in height. It had an opening at the bottom, large enough for him to crawl through; indeed, to his mind, it was there especially for the very use he intended to put it.

Running forward just as the rain began to rattle down all around him, Jerry proceeded to crawl through the aperture. He found the interior amply large enough to give him the needed shelter. What was better, the opening happened to be on the leeward side, so that the driving rain could not find entrance.

"This is what I call a bully fit. Talk to me about your cyclone cellars, what could beat such a cozy den as this? I'm as snug as a bug in a rug. Four wild dogs and my first deer, all in one day. I guess that's my top-notch record, all right. Let her storm all she wants, so long as the lightning doesn't take a notion to strike this blessed old stump," he was saying as he mentally shook hands with himself over the day's achievements.

After a long time, hours it seemed to Jerry, during a temporary lull in the howling of the gale, he ventured to peep forth.

Everything was pitch black around, save when the lightning zigzagged through space, and lighted up all creation with its electric torch.

"Looks like an all-night stand for Jerry. There comes that wind tearing things loose again. Wow! it was a big tree went down that time! Hope none of them take a notion to knock my poor old stump flat, or I'd be squashed
into a pancake."

Like many other people, Jerry had a habit of talking to himself under stress of excitement Perhaps he believed that in this way he bolstered up his courage, just as some men whistle when they find themselves trembling in the face of some uncanny peril.

And there he crouched while the gale blew with renewed violence, and the night wore slowly on. Several times there came a lull, and he began to hope the worst had passed; when once again the wind would swoop down, as though loth to give up its riotous dominion over the stricken forest.

Never had such a storm been heard of in October; even the first gale, which had demolished the roof of the Academy, and brought about this two weeks' vacation for the boys, had not equaled this, coming from another quarter as it did.

Jerry had one bad scare.

He had blocked up the entrance as best he could with what

stray bits of wood he found around. Suddenly he felt his barrier moving, and realized that some wild animal was nosing around, trying to force an entrance for shelter.

It must, after all, be the lair of a bear which he had found. Was this most remarkable day in all his experience to be wound up with an encounter that might dwarf the other into insignificance?

Jerry gave a shout. At the same time he seized upon his gun, and fired one barrel squarely through the opening. He thought he heard a loud "woof," but after that there was no further molestation.

But, nevertheless, he lay there wide-awake, and on his guard. Should Mr. Bear pluck up courage enough to return, he meant to be ready to give him a warm reception.

Time passed, and he believed the storm was really diminishing in fury. It was certainly time, for from the various crashes Jerry believed considerable timber must have gone to the ground.

How thankful he should be to have escaped as well as he had. Why, the mere fact that he was lost did not cut any figure in the matter when so many more terrible things might have happened to him.

There was really no sense of him leaving his snug retreat until dawn came, for he could not make his way in the storm-wrecked timber with any hope of success.

Again he poked his way out to take an observation. Perhaps he was wondering if his shot could have killed the bear; but no sign of such met his strained eyesight when the next flash of lightning came.

But while he was thus trying to pierce the gloom around him, he heard a sound that thrilled him through and through - the sound of a human voice calling.

"Help, oh! help!" it came wailing through the night.

CHAPTER XVI

HEAPING COALS OF FIRE ON HIS HEAD

"What's that?" exclaimed Jerry, startled by the cry.

It came again.

"Help! Oh! help, somebody!"

The boy was now convinced that he had not heard the hoot of an owl, and that some one was certainly in need of succor.

He remembered the crash of the trees that had gone down in the tempest. Could it be possible that the unfortunate one had been caught under one of these falling forest monarchs, and pinned to the ground?

If so, no wonder that he cried at the top of his voice for assistance. Unable to escape he must starve to death, or become the prey of wild beasts unless help came.

Jerry immediately crawled out of his hole. He no longer remembered the fact that a bear had recently been sniffing at the entrance to the hollow tree. All he had in mind was that he might be of assistance to a fellow human being in distress.

It was pitch dark in the woods, though now and then a flash of distant lightning came to momentarily relieve the gloom.

Jerry started in the direction he believed the sounds came from. Now and then he paused to listen, and in this way managed to keep going straight.

"Hello! where are you?" he cried, finally, as a dreadful silence fell upon the forest ahead, a silence that made him very anxious indeed.

Immediately a voice called out wildly:

"Oh, here I am, under this fallen tree! Please come and help me! I can't hardly move, and I think my arm is broken. Don't leave me to die!"

"It's all right. Don't worry, for I'm not going to run away. Speak again so I can get to you. It's awful dark under here."

The other took him at his word, and commenced to rattle on, saying all manner of things, simply to direct his rescuer to the spot.

"It's Andy Lasher, as sure as I live," said Jerry to himself, as he recognized the other's voice, despite the agony in it.

So making his way forward he finally came to the tree under which the other was pinioned by some of the branches.

"I can't see you, it's so dark here. Wait!" he said aloud.

"Oh! please don't leave me now; I'll go out of my mind, sure!"

"I don't mean to; but I must have some light. Now, I happen to have the stub of a candle in my pocket, and the wind has died out, so I think it will burn if I stick it down low. I'll get you out somehow, Andy," said Jerry, cheerily.

He struck a match.

"Why, is it you, Jerry?"

"Sure thing. See there, that burns all right, I guess. Now, I'll put it here in the shelter of this stump, while I look into things."

"You won't leave me here, Jerry? You ain't that kind of a feller, I know?"

Andy was evidently alarmed. He could not but remember that there had been bad blood between this lad and himself for a long time. Indeed, some recent events that were not at all to his credit, must have cropped up to make him anxious.

"Not much. Say, you just had the escape of your life, I tell you. This heavy limb almost hit you in falling. If it had, then it would have been one, two three for you. You seem to be held down mostly by small branches," observed Jerry, after he had made a critical examination.

"Do you think you can get me out, Jerry?" asked the other, very humbly.

"Easy. Just you wait, and when I tell you what to do, go ahead."

With that he started operations. By breaking off the smaller branches one at a time, he gradually weakened the network that was binding the prisoner. Every obstacle, however small, that was removed, made things easier. And finally Jerry gave a pull at the imprisoned boy.

Andy let out a howl of pain, but all the same he came free.

"My arm!"

"I'm going to look at that now, right away. If it is broken the sooner you get back to Centerville and see a doctor the better; but, somehow, I've got a notion it's only badly bruised. Here, bend it back, so I can slip it out of the sleeve."

With much misgiving and many exclamations of agony, Andy did as he was told. The other then examined it from one end to the other.

"Talk to me about luck, you've got cause to be mighty thankful, Andy. There are a lot of bruises here, but no bones broken," declared Jerry.

"Sure you ain't mistaken, Jerry - 'cause it's awful sore?" groaned the other, and yet there was a trace of gratitude in his voice.

"Make up your mind it's so. Now, the question is what are we going to do the rest of the night? I was in a hollow tree, but there isn't room fortwo. Might manage to make a fire somehow, and stand it out. Think you can walk now, Andy?"

Jerry unconsciously thrust a supporting arm around the waist of the other, and steadied his steps as they moved slowly off. In so doing he was heaping coals of fire upon the head of his adversary. Andy grunted now and then as some jolt gave him new pain; but on the whole he was very quiet. Perhaps his mind was busy and his conscience working overtime.

So they reached the hollow stump.

"Here's where I was camped all through the storm, and mighty lucky for you that I lost my way when out hunting. Now wait till I dig out some of that dry wood from the inside. It will make a capital start for a fire."

Jerry set to work with a vim. In five minutes he had a cheery little blaze going, and more wood drying out close beside it. From time to time other fuel was added to the fire until it reached such proportions that it eagerly devoured any sort of stuff they chose to feed it.

"This ain't half bad, because it's getting mighty cold after that storm, and if you happened to be lying drenched through under that tree I reckon you'd be shivering some by now, eh?" laughed Jerry.

Andy put out his right hand, for it was the left arm that had been injured.

"I want to tell you that I feel pretty punk now over the way I've treated your crowd, Jerry. This is mighty white in you, and that's what, to act as you have with me. I'm right sorry now I ever laid out to hurt you fellers. I ain't goin' to keep it up no longer, and that's dead certain. If Pet Peters wants to, he can go it alone. I'm all in. You've made me ashamed."

Jerry understood. There was really no need of further words. Between two boys such things are instinctively grasped; and Jerry knew what a tremendous effort it must have been for this rough fellow to frankly admit that he had been led to see the error of his ways.

Perhaps the repentance was not wholly genuine, and time would swing Andy back to his old ways; but just then, sitting by that friendly fire, he seemed to feel very warmly disposed toward the lad whose coming may have saved his life.

"Oh! that's all right; don't mention it. Glad to know you mean to let us alone. It's all we ask, anyway. But what brought you away up here, Andy?" said Jerry.

Andy dropped his head and gazed into the fire. The other even thought he could see what looked like a blush mantle his cheeks, though the chums of the town bully would have shouted at the very idea of such a thing.

"I reckon it was some more rotten business, Jerry. To tell the truth I was up to see old Bud Rabig, trying to get him to join us in a raid on your camp. You see," the boy went on hurriedly, as though fearful lest his courage might fail him before he got the whole thing off his mind, "we'd tried to smoke you out and made a botch of the trick; and I even pushed Bluff over into the lake this afternoon, to get him a duckin', 'cause the temptation was too great But it's all up with me now. After this I ain't goin' to lift a hand against any of your crowd."

"Did you get lost, too, trying to make your way back to your camp?" asked Jerry.

"That's just what I did. Thought I could save time by taking a short-cut through the big woods. Then the storm came down on me, and I reckon I got some rattled. I lost my head, and while I thrashed around, that pesky old tree came down on me. Thought I was a-goner, I give you my word," and Andy shuddered.

"How long did you lie there?" questioned the other.

"Hours and hours, it seemed to me. I'd shout when I could, but something seemed to tell me it wasn't no good - that I just deserved to die right there, because I'd never been no good to my folks at home or anybody else. But you just wait and see. I got a light, I did. Thought I was sure goin' to die."

Both boys were soon sleepy, for the heat of the fire affected their eyes. So Jerry fixed things to keep the blaze going while they napped, rolling a log over so that it offered a good chance for the fire to feed.

In this way they passed the balance of the night, nor would either of them soon forget the experience, though from different reasons.

In the morning they managed to cook some of the fresh venison Jerry carried, and for which the other seemed very grateful. Then they figured out their position, which was not hard to do, since the sky was clear and the sun well up.

Half an hour later Andy recognized certain landmarks that told him he could make a turn and reach his camp by the lake shore.

"Good-by, Jerry. I'm going to skip out here. And I ain't forgettin' this either," he said, thrusting out a hand, while a queer grin crept over his face.

Jerry hurried on, anxious to relieve the suspense of his chums.

As he came in sight of the camp he paused and stared, as well he might, for it seemed to be occupied by a stranger, and he a man with the wild aspect of a madman.

CHAPTER XVII

AFTER THE STORM

"Whoop! All hands on deck to pump ship!"

"My camera! Oh! where did I put it?"

"Grab up the bedding and hustle in under the other tent, boys!"

This last from steady, clear-headed Frank, who seemed to know just what should be done in an emergency.

It started Bluff and Uncle Toby working strenuously to keep blankets from getting very wet. But Will could not think of lending a hand until he had first of all lugged his beloved camera under shelter.

It was indeed fortunate that both tents had not gone by the board at the same time, or the camp must have been plunged into the deepest distress. Led by Frank, they managed to hustle their belongings under the second cover, where the driving rain could not reach them.

By the time all had been done the boys were dripping, and it took them some twenty minutes to get warm again, snuggled in their blankets.

"Oh! what a night!" wailed Will a dozen times.

"Please let up on that, or give us a change in tune. It's bad enough to have to stand the storm without listening to a phonograph," grunted Bluff.

The hours crept along. Now and then they dozed, but sound slumber did not come to a single one of the group. Uncle Toby was quite content to cower as close to Frank as possible, satisfied that the other was able to protect him. He seemed to exhibit the blind confidence of a dog in an emergency calling for energy; to him Frank was a type of manliness hard to match.

"Will the morning ever come?" groaned Will, as he shifted his cramped position for the tenth time at least.

"Well, I think we've got a lot to be thankful for," declared Frank, stoutly; "in the first place, no great damage is done, for I saw that our tent was caught in the branches of a tree close by, and we can rescue it in the morning. Then nothing was spoiled that I know of. And the storm is really over, though morning is some two hours off," striking a match and looking at his nickel watch.

"Can't we have a fire?" asked Will, who was shivering under his blanket.

"Just thinking so myself. It's getting sharp, now that the wind has shifted into the northwest. Suppose we make a try," answered Frank, readily.

It was just in anticipation of such an emergency that he had hidden some of the dry wood away where the rain could not reach it. Frank's previous experience in woodcraft had taught him many valuable things.

Securing some of this, he quickly had a little blaze. The others fed this in a cautious manner, so as not to smother it by too much fuel. As a result the fire was in a short time burning freely, and diffusing a genial warmth around that proved very acceptable to the chilled campers.

Even Will thawed out under its influence and ceased to grumble.

"It's all right, too, fellows; not a drop got in tinder these waterproofs," he declared, as he eagerly examined his precious possession.

So the morning found them.

The first thing they did was to rescue the runaway canvas. It was found to be intact, the pins only having given under the strain. So shortly afterwards the second tent again arose, and things began to look shipshape around the camp.

"Seems like an Irish wash-day," remarked Will, as he surveyed the various blankets and other things spread out on bushes to dry in the sunshine and air.

"Only for Jerry's strange absence, I'd feel bully," remarked Frank.

"Don't you think we'd better start out and look for him?" asked Will.

"Yes, after we've had some breakfast. I never like to attempt anything on an empty stomach. And, besides, you see, we may have to go all the way over to Jesse's shack before we learn about him," observed Frank.

"Do you really think he's stayed there?" questioned Bluff, anxiously; for even though he and Jerry seemed to be constantly bickering, deep down in their hearts they had a genuine affection for each other, as had been proven more than once.

"I hope so," was all the other would say.

"And I've got a dreadful fear," remarked Will, sighing, "that the poor fellow's been caught under a falling tree. So many went down last night. I'll hear that terrible crashing every time I wake up for a long time to come. It haunts me, just because I imagined Jerry out in it all."

Toby here banged the big spoon on the empty frying pan. That was a welcome sound to a set of ravenous boys, and they quickly assembled around the rude table upon which the black *chef* was placing heaps of flapjacks, flanked by steaming cups of fragrant coffee.

Uncle Toby did not seem to relish being left alone in the camp again; but there was nothing else to be done. Frank gave him some advice as to what he should do if any wild beast invaded the place; and also how he could threaten any of Andy's crowd should they show up with hostile intent.

Then the three boys started off, meaning to head in a direct line for the distant camp of the old trapper.

"What if we don't find him there?" asked the skeptical Will.

"Wait till we get to the river before trying to cross. I reckon we'll be apt to find some traces of him there. And even if he was caught out in the woods in that storm, that's no sign he was hurt or killed. Jerry knows enough to get in out of the wet; and depend on it he found shelter somehow, somewhere."

So Frank buoyed their spirits up in his accustomed cheery way. One could easily see that he belonged to the optimist family, and never looked on the gloomy side of things.

They had not gone half a mile away from the camp before they discovered some one moving through the bushes ahead.

"There he is!" exclaimed Bluff, eagerly, as he raised his hand to his mouth, as if about to give a "cooie."

"Hold on! I don't believe it is. There, you see, it's a man, and a hunter, too, I expect, for he's carrying a gun," interrupted Frank.

"Perhaps he may have seen Jerry. Shall we ask him?" demanded Will.

"If we keep on straight we're going to meet him, and, of course, we'll ask. I only hope he has, though I doubt it. Do either of you know him?"

Frank asked this because he was comparatively a newcomer in Centerville, while the other boys had been raised there.

"Seems to me I've seen him before," exclaimed Bluff. "Why, yes, it's Mr. Smithson. He lives in Centerville - that is, his family does, because he isn't home much. You see he's one of the wardens over at the State insane asylum at Merrick."

"What?" cried Frank, startled; "then perhaps he may not be hunting wild animals after all. Suppose one of the mad inmates of that institution escaped, and is up here roaming through the woods?"

"Jewhittaker!" exclaimed Will, turning a trifle pale, and hugging his camera closer to his breast, as though his first fear concerned its safety.

"If that's so, I hope Jerry didn't run across him, that's all," remarked Bluff.

"Come on, hurry. You've given me a little shock now, and we must learn the truth immediately. Call out to him, Bluff - there, he sees us, and is coming this way."

As Frank said, the keeper was hurrying toward them now, an anxious look on his face. He nodded to Bluff as he came up.

"Camping up here, are you, boys? That's fine. Used to like to do it myself when I was younger. Say, you didn't happen to see anything of a wild-looking chap anywhere around, did you?" he asked, glancing at each in turn.

"Sorry to say we haven't, Mr. Smithson. Has one of your charges got away?"

"That's just what has happened, and I've been chasing him all over the country. Got track of him yesterday just before the beastly old storm hit me. He's somewhere around this section right now. Where's your camp, boys? He'll be pretty sharp set with hunger by now, and can scent grub a long ways off?" continued the keeper.

The three lads looked at each other.

"What shall we do, fellows? Doesn't seem just right to be chasing off this way in a bunch, and leaving that poor old innocent alone in camp. What if this crazy man drops in on Toby while we're gone? Had we better turn back, and later on, if Jerry doesn't show up, organize another expedition, dividing our forces?"

Frank always put things so clearly that he seldom met with any opposition.

"That strikes me as sensible," observed Will, quickly.

"Turn back it is, then. Will you go with us, Mr. Smithson? We can give you a good cup of hot coffee, and some breakfast, if you're hungry?" said Bluff.

"I accept your offer, boys, and glad to meet you. Now, lead the way, please, because somehow, I seem to feel it in my bones that Bismarck will gravitate toward some place where there is an odor of cookery in the air. He always was a good feeder."

"Bismarck?" ejaculated Frank.

"Why, you see, that's what he thinks, and he carries out the part to a dot. Wait till you run up against him, if luck turns that way," replied the other.

"He may have been injured in the storm?" suggested Will.

"Not he. Such a cunning fellow would know how to escape a wet back."

"Is he considered dangerous?" Bluff inquired, a little anxiously.

"Well, not particularly, although he can look mighty fierce, and would terrify a timid person, possibly."

"And I guess Uncle Toby fills that bill, all right," said Bluff; "but there's our camp through the trees, Mr. Smithson; and, as sure as you live, there's a stranger standing poking at the fire where our cook is bending down."

"Bismarck is making himself at home, all right," laughed the warden.

CHAPTER XVIII

A STRANGE VISITOR IN CAMP

"What can we do about it?" asked Will, looking alarmed.

"It's up to Mr. Smithson," remarked Frank, in a low tone.

"Look here, boys, you understand that I want to capture the gentleman very much indeed. Are you willing to give me a little assistance?" asked the warden.

"Why, to be sure we will. It looks as though we might have some interest in his capture, too, judging by the way old Toby is loading up our good grub in those frying pans to suit his appetite. He threatens to eat us out of house and home unless something desperate is done. We'll help capture the escaped lunatic, eh, fellows?"

"Sure we will, Frank. Let Mr. Smithson tell us what to do, that's all," said Bluff, readily.

"Well, I hardly think he'll take the alarm at sight of any strangers, so long as he doesn't get a glimpse of me. Now, if you three just saunter easily into camp, and pretend to treat him in a friendly way, you'll find he can be a fine gentleman. Humor his failing as much as you can, boys."

"And what else, sir?" asked Frank, who was listening intently.

"Meanwhile I'll be creeping closer all the while. After he has been fed he may feel sleepy, because he must have been up all night. The heat of the fire and a good feed will make his eyes heavy," continued Mr. Smithson.

"I guess you're right, sir."

"Very good. Suppose you propose that he lie down by the fire and take a nap. Rig him up a sort of military bed. He imagines that Bismarck is with the old emperor, off in France on the war campaign. When he's fast asleep I'll creep into camp and get him secure. It will be easy, boys, believe me."

"Say, is he the only one loose?" asked Will, just then, his voice showing alarm.

"Why, yes, so far as I know. Why do you ask?" demanded the warden.

"Because there's some one else crawling through the bushes over yonder."

"Are you sure?" asked Mr. Smithson.

"I saw his head pop up. He's looking in at our camp. Get your gun ready, Frank. Some of these crazy people are said to be dangerous," continued Will.

"Humbug! If you saw any one at all it must have been a scout from Andy Lasher's camp, snooping around," commented Bluff, disdainfully.

"Well, perhaps it might be another keeper from the asylum," remarked Smithson.

"There it is again; what did I tell you, fel - "

Will stopped speaking in a whisper and gaped. True enough a human head had bobbed up above the tops of the bushes, as the owner of the same endeavored to get a better view of the camp.

"It's Jerry!" ejaculated Bluff, in excitement.

Mr. Smithson dropped out of sight, thinking that the stranger in camp might look that way, being attracted by the clamor of boyish tongues. Jerry had caught the words of Bluff and immediately turned his head.

"Hello, fellows! Howdye? And who under the sun is the new manager you've got to run the camp?" he asked, pushing out to greet them each in turn, and eyeing Mr. Smithson in some curiosity.

"How are you, Jerry? Guess you know me all right, eh? Why, I'm up here looking for an escaped lunatic, you see," said that worthy, without rising.

"Talk to me about your coincidences - and that's him right there in our camp, ordering poor old scared Uncle Toby around with the air of an emperor. I see it all, boys," exclaimed Jerry, shaking hands around as though he had been gone for a full week instead of one night.

"Well, he believes himself a bigger man than any emperor, for he makes and unmakes kings. That is Bismarck you see, young man. And we have just been laying a plan to capture him. Suppose you all saunter into camp now. Somebody tell Jerry what we have decided to do. He's looking this way, and ready to either run or hold his ground according to how the wind blows."

"Come on, Jerry. You can tell us all that happened later. We must get rid of this unwelcome visitor first," said Frank.

"We had just started out to learn what had become of you when we met Mr. Smithson, and he advised us to return to our camp, as he rather expected the gentleman he was looking for would drift that way. Awful glad you got through that terrible storm safe, old chap," remarked Will.

"What are those things tied in a bunch at your belt - scalps?" queried Bluff, as they walked along together.

"The tails of four wild dogs that tackled me in the big timber after I had shot a deer which they wanted," remarked Jerry, trying to speak naturally.

"What!" exclaimed the others in concert.

"Oh, it's a positive fact, boys. I can take you to where the critters lie, if you want to see them later. I was told about them ranging that section, by Jesse, who warned me to look out for them. I met the pack all right, and I guess they wished I hadn't. Here's some of the fresh venison. I hung up most of it so we could get it later. Then we made a breakfast on part of what I was lugging home," Jerry went on.

"We?" remarked Frank, inquiringly.

"Of course. Andy Lasher and myself."

"Andy Lasher! Where did you run across *him*, and how did it come that you let that miserable skunk eat breakfast with you?" demanded Bluff.

"Well, he was in a bad way, you see. I just happened to get him out from under the branches of a fallen tree that had him pinned tight to the ground. His arm was bruised, and we bunked together until morning. Andy's got a repentant mood on him. He vows he's done playing nasty tricks on our club. 'Course I don't know how it will pan out, boys."

"Say, did he tell you anything about my gun?" asked Bluff, eagerly.

Jerry turned and looked at the questioner.

"No, he didn't. Suppose he confessed to everything he ever did? But here we are, fellows, and our guest looks as if he didn't know whether to run for it or hang by that breakfast Toby is cooking."

Frank advanced toward the man, bowing, and assuming, as he believed, something of a military air.

"Welcome to our camp, Prince Bismarck. Won't you be seated, and wait for breakfast to be served? We have only rude accommodations here, but I hope you will pardon any lack of seeming hospitality," he said.

The wild look vanished from the face of the gaunt man, and in its place came an expression of tremendous importance. Indeed, but for the seriousness of the situation Frank would have felt inclined to laugh outright, it was so absurd to see this poor lunatic putting on such magnificent airs.

"You forget, young sir, that I am the Iron Chancellor, and that while in the field I shun all the comforts of home life. An iron cot, the simplest food, these are enough for me. It leaves the brain clear to handle the tremendous affairs of state that engross our attention. Where is King William?" the other went on.

"Oh, he'll be along after awhile. Perhaps, prince, after you have partaken of our simple fare and rested by our friendly fire a little time, the king may join you."

Frank managed to keep a sober face while speaking in this lofty way, but Bluff and Jerry, unable to stand it any longer, turned their backs on the couple.

Evidently the lunatic was very hungry, in spite of his possession of an "iron will." He kept turning a wistful eye toward the fire where the frightened black cook was hustling coffee and ham and eggs for his benefit. And indeed, there was such an appetizing odor in the air that several times Mr.

Smithson raised his head and looked longingly over the bushes as though he wished things would move faster, so he could come into camp and get his share.

When the food was placed before him the man ate ravenously. The boys afterwards learned that he had not tasted a bite for two days, and they wondered at his having shown even as much patience as he did.

Just as Mr. Smithson had said, the escaped lunatic became drowsy as soon as he finished eating.

"Let me fix a nice cot for you here, prince. When the king arrives you shall be awakened, all right," said Frank, soothingly.

The man looked trustingly at him, so that Frank felt a little qualm of conscience over the fact that he had to deceive him.

"You are very kind, young sir. Indeed, I believe I am weary, and perhaps a nap would refresh me. If Napoleon sends out a flag of truce notify me at once," and he settled down on the warm blankets with a sigh of pleasure.

"Depend on it, such shall be done," replied Frank, turning away; for he had by this time reached the limit of his endurance, and if compelled to keep this thing up much longer must have betrayed himself by laughter.

In ten minutes he flew a handkerchief as a signal that the warden could come in.

Mr. Smithson grinned as he joined them.

"It was well done, my boy. You would sure make an actor, all right. And now, for fear lest he slip me, I'll have to nab him," he said.

"Do you want any help, sir?" queried Frank.

"Oh! I reckon not. When he sees that I've got him he'll be as meek as a lamb. He looks on me as a jealous German general desirous of keeping him out of touch with the king. Watch now."

He bent over the sleeper and touched his face.

"Wake up, Prince Bismarck," he said, in a commanding tone.

The other opened his eyes, stared and then smiled amiably, saying:

"Oh! it's you, is it, general? Fate is against me again. I yield myself a prisoner of war. You can fasten my hands if you wish, but I have dined well for one day."

CHAPTER XIX

SURPRISING TRAPPER JESSE

Mr. Smithson had carried his prisoner off, after he, too, had partaken of the hospitality of Kamp Kill Kare.

"Boys," he said, in leaving, "I'm sure under obligations to you for all this, and any time I can repay the debt don't hesitate to ask me. To get Bismarck back safe and sound after such a storm, is going to be a feather in my cap. And only for you I'd be hunting him yet, with only a slim chance of success."

"Why, that's all right, Mr. Smithson," Frank had declared heartily; "we've enjoyed helping you, though it does make a fellow feel bad to see as clever a man as that laboring under such a ridiculous fancy."

"He was once a professor in a college, and lost his mind through overstudy," remarked the keeper, as he moved off, with "Bismarck" at his side.

"There, see that!" exclaimed Bluff, triumphantly. "Just what I've told my dad many a time when he complained that I was falling behind my class. I'll make certain to hold this up as an awful warning."

"Talk to me about you losing your brain by overstudy! There's about as much chance of that as my being made king of England," laughed Jerry.

"But still it *has* happened, you see. That establishes a precedent all right, and my father, as a lawyer, is always talking about such things," declared Bluff, not in the least abashed.

"Now suppose you sit right down here, Jerry, and let us have the whole yarn from Alpha to Omega. What you haven't been through since you left us yesterday morning isn't worth mentioning, to judge from the hints you let fall. A deer, four wild dogs, lost in the big timber, storm bound, rescuing our most bitter enemy; and now helping to land an escaped lunatic - say, you ought to feel satisfied, old fellow," observed Frank.

Jerry laughed aloud.

All his recent troubles, as viewed from the pleasant seat by the campfire, with his three chums around him, seemed to fade into insignificance.

"Well, I reckon I am. There was a bear, too," he said, nodding.

"What! a bear - you ran across a bear?" ejaculated Will, drawing in a big breath and shaking this head as if he deplored the loss of an opportunity to embellish his album of the camping-out trip with more fetching views.

"Well, perhaps you could hardly call it that, seeing that he came looking for me, trying to push into the hollow tree where I had sought shelter from the storm."

"That sounds mighty interesting - trying to get in, too, was he? And I suppose you objected vigorously?" suggested Frank, falling down by the fire and assuming a listening attitude.

"I knew I hadn't lost any bear, you see; and, besides, there wasn't room for two in that old stump. So I asked him to please go away," said Jerry, with a wink.

"Of course he did just that?" queried Will.

"After I had shouted, and fired my gun through the hole. He was somewhat surprised at such a rude reception, for I guess that stump was one of his dens, and he thought he had the first claim on it."

"Well, start in now with your getting over at the camp of Jesse, and give us all the thrills you want. You've got proof about the deer and the wild dogs; but perhaps we'll have to consider the story about the bear," laughed Frank.

"And Andy Lasher's repentance; that is the most surprising of all," declared Bluff, shaking his head as though he could not understand it at all.

They sat there spellbound while Jerry skimmed over the entire account of his adventures since quitting the camp. As the reader already knows what befell him, it would be useless repeating the story. The three chums, however, listened and exchanged looks with one another as some particularly thrilling incident came along, as though they could imagine Jerry facing that big yellow brute that chased him round and round the tree until he was dizzy enough to drop ere he remembered that he had a gun in his hand.

"I move we go out there right after lunch and get the balance of the venison. We may not have another chance to lay in a stock of fresh meat all the time we're up here," proposed Will, finally.

"Oh! I can see that you're doubting my story about the dogs, and wondering where under the sun I ran across these four tails. All right, fellows, I'll do the best I can to take you to the place. Perhaps if we went to old Jesse he could guide us there much better," declared the mighty hunter, calmly.

"He talks as though he courts an investigation," remarked Frank; "and in justice to his reputation, I think we ought to settle this matter without delay. So I'm in favor of going, for one; besides, I confess to a curiosity to see the dead dogs, and, perhaps, if fate is kind, look into the identical hollow tree in which Jerry passed most of that stormy night."

"It's a go, then," cried Will, eagerly; "for I want a few more pictures. If we could only rig up something to look like that yellow hound, and have Jerry galloping around that tree in front of him, it would be simply immense."

"Talk to me about a faker will you - why, if Will keeps on he'll be bamboozling the public worse than any showman ever did. Thanks, but I guess you'll have to excuse me from that galloping act, Will. Once bit, twice shy, you know. But it was gospel truth about Andy. He even confessed that he had been up to old Rabig's place to get him to join the crowd in playing some more measly tricks on us here. You see he was sorry, and had to just tell all these things."

"All but about my gun, hang him," grumbled Bluff, indignantly.

"Bother your old gun! Will we ever hear the last of it?" exclaimed Jerry, frowning; and yet giving Frank a sly wink with one eye, as if to inform him that he did not really mean all he said.

"You never heard the first of it yet, for I didn't even have a single chance to shoot it off," complained the other.

"For which all the little birds and chipmunks are rejoicing, for they have had a chance to live. Besides, a gun like that is dangerous to the community, I think. If it ever started to going I believe it would spit out fire without any help from you, or any one else. But, for goodness' sake, change the subject. I'm sleepy," declared Jerry, curling up on a blanket by the fire.

"All of us are, I reckon. You see we were having a little circus of our own at the time this happened to you," remarked Frank.

"Yes," exclaimed Bluff, " don't you think you're the only

pebble on the beach, Jerry."

"Why, what happened?" demanded the other, looking up.

"Why, what do you think we've got all those things on the bushes drying out for? Yes, one of the tents blew away in the middle of the storm. I think it must have been an hour or two before midnight, when the big gust came that tore it loose. We were all four of us under it, and there was some tall scurrying just then, believe me."

"I can well believe it, Frank. Where was Will with his camera then?" asked Jerry.

"Trying to keep the blessed thing from getting soaked," answered Bluff.

"Then he doesn't believe in wet plates?" laughed the other.

"Seems not; films are good enough for him. Well, we managed to get all the things under the shelter of the other tent, and shivered for some hours. Finally, after the storm passed, and it began to get very cold, we started a fire and waited to welcome the rosy dawn."

"Don't get poetic, Frank. I'm really too dead for sleep to appreciate it now. Wake me up, fellows, when lunch is ready, will you?" and, so speaking, Jerry curled up again, this time in earnest.

The others amused themselves the balance of the morning in various ways. Bluff declared that he believed he would stay in camp while the others went off. Frank looked at him curiously as if wondering what had struck him, for he considered that the trip was well worth taking, if only to see the husky-looking wild dogs Jerry had met and slain.

He could remember having heard one or two persons speaking about the pack that was giving the farmers so much trouble.

To think that, after all, their comrade had been the one to relieve the situation, was pleasant indeed.

They aroused Jerry when Uncle Toby announced that lunch was ready. The old man seemed to be kept pretty busy preparing meals for all stragglers happening in; but that part of the business pleased him. The only thing he protested against was being left alone in camp. There were too many visitors at such times to suit him.

First had come the wildcat, and then the wild man. Uncle Toby had therefore heard Bluff's announcement that he intended remaining behind when the others went off, with particular pleasure and much relief.

Immediately afterwards the three lads started out. Jerry seemed much refreshed by his nap, and was as lively as either of his comrades.

A straight line was kept for the shack of the old trapper, and when they finally reached the place it was to find Jesse just starting out.

"Why, hello, boys, glad to see ye," he said, shaking hands all around, gravely. "And I'll be hanged, if thar ain't Jerry, big as life. I was gettin' uneasy about ye, lad, an' just startin' to follow up your route through the big timber. Ye see, I kinder thought ye might a-fallen foul o' them fierce wild dogs I told ye about."

Both Frank and Will laughed.

"Well, he did all right, just that same thing. And we're on our way now to see where he left the critters," declared Will.

"Left 'em - looky here, ye don't mean to tell me - it can't be possible now he fit that hull pack, an' got out o' it alive?" exclaimed the trapper.

Then Jerry, with a laugh, dangled the four tails before his startled eyes.

CHAPTER XX

PROVING HIS CLAIM

"Jerusalem! I surely believes he's gone an' done it!" exclaimed old Jesse Wilcox.

Frank and Will burst out into a laugh.

"Do you recognize these tails then, trapper?" asked the former; "because we even accused Jerry of trying to palm off some substitute on us for the originals?"

"Oh! them there is original tails all right. How did ye do it, youngster? An' if they ever was fierce dogs, that pack filled the bill. I'd kinder hated to be up agin 'em myself; an' you on'y a boy!"

"A boy armed with a double-barreled shotgun loaded with buck is able to do just as much as a man, I suppose. I got my deer, too, Jesse, thanks to the directions you gave me. It was a bully old time all around," said Jerry, contentedly.

"Well, I should smile to mention it. Ye take the cake, Jerry. An' now ye want me to lead ye thar, I s'pose. Can ye describe the place well enough for me to recognize it?" asked the trapper.

"Possibly I can. Let's see, I remember that there was a queer-looking oak standing close by - three trees in one, as though sprouts had grown up when the parent trunk was smashed by lightning long ago. Remember having seen anything like that in your trips through the big timber, Jesse?" asked the other, seriously.

The trapper smiled.

"Why, it's right easy. I know that place as well as I do my own dooryard. Shot a stag down by them three oaks myself ten years ago come Christmas. So that's whar ye met up with the dog pack, was it? All right, if so be ye are ready, we kin start right off," he remarked eagerly.

All of the others were equally anxious to proceed, Jerry because he wished to prove his hunting triumphs, and his chums to see the evidence of his valor. Will, no doubt, still hoped to induce the victor to attempt some sort of running stunt in connection with the tree and the dead dogs, that would form the basis of a striking picture.

Going in a bee line, as led by the sagacious trapper, who knew the woods like a book, the little company did not spend more than an hour on the way.

"Thar's yer three oaks, son; now tell us jest whar ye was when ye shot that deer."

As he spoke, Jesse pointed ahead. All of them could easily see the landmark now.

"It was an old tree, and there ought to be broken branches underneath. Yes, if you look over yonder you'll see it. And isn't there something that looks yellow from here?" asked Jerry, proudly.

"Just what! The dog story was founded on solid facts, then!" exclaimed Frank, hurrying forward, with the others at his heels.

"It was a true tale," chimed in Will, from the rear.

They found the dogs just as Jerry had left them. The big yellow brute lay under the rotten tree, with his head mangled from the discharge of the gun at close quarters; the dingy white one farther off, and presently Jerry led them to where he had dispatched the others.

"And there's my package of vension, all right, hanging up yonder. I was afraid some prowling lynx might get away with it," he remarked, composedly; while his two admiring chums were whacking him on the back admiringly, and insisting on proudly shaking hands with him over and over again.

"Now, to make a clean sweep, come with me and I'll show you where I pulled Andy out from under the fallen tree," he said.

Frank laughed and would have protested, declaring that he stood ready to believe anything Jerry might say after this; but the other would not let him hold back.

"I demand that you investigate. See, here's where my charge tore up the ground when I fired through the rotten wood to scare the bear away. And you can see the plain mark of claws on the old tree-trunk. Is it so, fellows?" he asked.

"Without the least doubt. No Ananias here, that's sure," declared Frank.

"All right. Now walk this way only a short distance. I heard the yells, you see, above the racket of the storm, and that told me the one who shouted must be near by. There's the fallen tree. Think what a narrow escape Andy had from being crushed to death."

"And it's easy to see where you dragged him out. Why, here are the prints of his shoes in the mud as plain as type," remarked Frank.

"Where?" asked Will, showing sudden interest; and then after getting down to look at short range he laughed, saying: "Everything is just as Jerry says. I know it was Andy he pulled out from under this tree."

"How do you know?" demanded the party in question, curiously.

"Why, you see it was Andy Lasher who knocked Bluff off that log into the lake. We guessed it at the time, and he afterwards said as much to Jerry here. Well, we found his footprints, and you see one of his shoes had a queer patch on the sole, a sort of triangle. Here it is, as big as life!"

He pointed triumphantly downward. Frank fairly shouted, and even Jerry grinned.

"Talk about your great detectives! Why, they ain't in the same class as our chum here. You see, fellows, truth will out. What more proof do you want?" demanded Jerry.

"Everything has been proven. You are the hero of the hunt, Jerry. I pass up my claim when you're around. And so Andy means to let us alone, does he? Can he speak for his whole crowd, too?" queried Frank.

"I don't know; perhaps not He said something about Pet Peters having to do it himself if he insisted on carrying on this nasty business of bothering us. So perhaps we may have more trouble with them, unless Andy takes the bit in his teeth, and licks a few of his pals."

Will was meanwhile busily engaged with his camera. He first of all dragged several of the dead dogs around until they presented a gruesome appearance, bunched close together.

"Oh, if you would only run around that old tree a few times, Jerry, you don't know how much obliged I'd be. Of course any one must imagine that the dog pursuing you happens to just be out of sight at the time I snap you off. But think how much pleasure the picture will give future generations. *Please* do!" he begged.

"What do I care about future generations? It would give me the nightmare every time I looked at the measly thing. I guess you'd feel the same way if you just imagined you were going to have a piece gobbled from your leg with every revolution you made. Nixey for me, old chum," observed the other, indignantly.

"Then if you won't, I suppose I'll have to take a still picture; but it's really too bad. However, I have others of you, and some day I'll try a composite picture, inserting you in the honorable position you decline to fill," grumbled Will, as he pressed the button, and secured his view of the venerable tree with the clump of dogs near its base.

"Talk about your obstinate chaps, did you ever see the equal of him? When I decline to do the tall running act, he's going to get out a fake picture anyway, with me in it! In that case I might as well stand for it. Here, you, I'll conspire with you to fix it. If it's got to be a counterfeit, let's make it a decent one."

So, after all, Will's persistency won out.

"You'll be glad when you see the result, I'm sure," he said, as he assisted Jerry to stand the dead hound on his stiffened feet, and make it appear as though he might be stretching out in furious pursuit of some one.

"Now, let me get started winding up around the tree. Tell me when the humbug business is over with," growled Jerry, beginning to circulate over the same track he had covered on the preceding day at such a speedy pace.

This matter was soon adjusted to the complete satisfaction of Will; though he seemed determined to get results, judging from the several "clicks" that announced his rapid-fire work with the camera.

The boys decided that there was no need of going back to the shack of the muskrat trapper again, while they were just half the distance from their own camp.

Jesse Wilcox directed them, so that there was small chance of their going astray; and, besides, Jerry had been over the ground before on this very morning.

"I wonder whether he'll bother taking the pelts of those four dogs?" ventured Will, as he and his two friends walked briskly along.

"Hardly. Dogskins may be valuable, but the buckshot in my gun just about ruined those for any use, all but the yellow fellow. I had to laugh at Jesse when he saw these tails. His eyes were like saucers," declared Jerry, chuckling.

"All right, it was a pretty clever piece of work, and he knew it. If that big hound had ever laid hold of you - ugh! I don't want to think of it. Let's talk about something pleasant - Bluff's pump-gun for instance," remarked Frank.

His eyes met those of Jerry, and the other turned red in the face.

"I don't see anything pleasant about that subject. Goodness knows we hear enough of it from him. What d'ye suppose he wanted to stay in camp for?" he demanded.

"Perhaps to cudgel his brains in order to remember whether he could have taken it with him when we ran out of camp that night; or, perhaps, to give another look around," suggested Frank, dryly.

"Good luck to him, then," continued Jerry. "He ought to employ the great American detective Will here, who discovers things by the print of a foot. Possibly he could follow up the trail of the thief until it led to the lost Gatling gun."

"It would have been a good idea if taken at the time. What's this plain trail lead to?" asked Frank.

"I think it leads direct from the hemlock camp to where Andy's crowd holds out," replied Jerry, who knew considerable about this region.

"Are we far away from the lake, then?"

"It's some closer than our camp. This trail has been traveled more or less lately, too. That proves those fellows have been back and forth. They're bound to spend pretty much all their time while up here trying to make life miserable for us. We turn to the left here, fellows, and go right along this way."

The other two, after a look along the trail that led to the lake camp, were just starting to follow Jerry when they heard a muffled cry. Looking hastily around, to their great astonishment no Jerry was in sight! And in the trail they discovered a gaping hole which was partly covered with a layer of slender sticks, thickly strewn with dead leaves!

CHAPTER XXI

DOWN THE OLD SHAFT

"He's gone!" cried Will, aghast.

"What sort of a trap has he dropped into?" exclaimed Frank.

He was a lad of action, and throwing himself down flat he crawled to the very edge of the gaping hole.

"Hello, Jerry!" he shouted.

"I'm all right, fellows; only bruised a little, and my feelings considerably hurt. I deserve something for forgetting this hole," came a voice from out of the depths.

Frank looked down. His eyes being accustomed to the sunlight he could not see anything but darkness there. But even as he was trying to pierce this, a match flamed up, and he discovered his chum kneeling on a pile of dirt, holding up his improvised torch as though curious to look around.

"What is this place, Jerry?" demanded the one above.

"Why, Will must remember if he once gets his mind off that miserable old camera of his. It's the shaft of what was intended to be a mine," replied Jerry, with disgust plainly marked in his tones.

"A mine - and here? I never heard of it!" echoed Frank.

"That's because you are a newcomer in Centerville. Years ago - oh! I couldn't say how many - a crank lived in the little hut close by, now occupied by the family of a lumberman. He believed there was gold in this region. For nearly a year he dug down and made this shaft. Then he died in his cabin, and no one else ever had faith enough in the thing to continue the work," said Will, chiming in.

"What! do you mean to say this hole in the ground has gone all these years as a trap, ready to swallow any pilgrim who walked along this trail?" demanded Frank.

"Why, of course not. The boys from town often used to come up here. Will has been down in this hole, and so have I before. It was covered with heavy planks then. Somebody has removed those boards and laid a fine trap. Just like we were over in Africa, among the wild-beast catchers. And I fell in, worse luck," grumbled the boy at the bottom of the shaft.

"I see. And you think those fellows in the other camp had a hand in it?"

"Don't doubt it at all. You know yourself it would be just like that Pet Peters. If I'd only thought of the blooming old thing in time, I might have investigated. Talk to me about your Alpine climbers, I thought I was going into the crevasse, all right."

"But how are you going to get out?" asked Frank, always practical.

"A fellow can't climb out. I know that, for we used to try it. Somebody always had to put down the long pole that we made into a ladder," declared Will.

"Is it around here now?" continued Frank.

"Wait and I'll give a look."

Will very carefully placed his camera with its accompanying case of films. He made sure that it was out of the way, so that no one might incautiously step on the same, and ruin his heart's delight. Then he passed into the bushes to scour the immediate neighborhood.

Meanwhile Frank bent over the edge again.

"I've examined this covering up here, Jerry, and there's not the least doubt but that it was made with a distinct purpose," he declared.

"I reckon it was, and it got me, all right. It looked just like the rest of the trail, and I never suspected a thing until I found myself going down. Speak to me about that, will you? To think that I was caught by such a shabby trick. If it had been you, now, it wouldn't seem so bad, because you never saw this hole before."

"But what object could those rascals have had in constructing the trap?" pursued Frank, seeking more light.

"That's hard to say. I imagine, though, they expected to just badger us from time to time until finally we all set out in full chase of the crowd. Then perhaps they meant to lead us along this old trail, avoiding the pit themselves, and having us tumble in pell-mell. It was a clever dodge, but a mean trick all the same."

"But if that had happened it might have been serious. One of us could easily break a leg or an arm in such a tumble," expostulated Frank.

"Huh! little those fellows care about that They're a rough lot, you know. That Pet Peters thinks everybody is made of iron, like himself. Say, I hope Will finds that old ladder we used to play with. I'd hate to lie in here waiting for you to go all the way to camp and get a rope," grumbled the imprisoned one.

"I hear voices, and I reckon Will must have met some one. Yes, there they come."

"With the ladder?" demanded Jerry, eagerly.

"They seem to be carrying something between them. Why, I ought to know that fellow. As sure as you live, it's Andy Lasher," declared Frank, somewhat surprised.

"Then it's all right; I'm satisfied," said Jerry, resignedly.

The others came forward, and as Frank had said they bore between them a long, slender tree upon which many slats had been nailed by the boys. This formed a rude but effective ladder, upon which one might ascend and descend when desirous of seeing what the interior of the abandoned shaft was like.

"I came across Andy down the trail. Only for him I guess I'd never have lit on the ladder, for they'd carried it some distance off, and hid it," cried Will.

Andy looked Frank straight in the face, and the latter explained:

"It's mighty funny, but you see I remembered about this here trap the boys had set, hopin' some of your crowd would take a tumble. I told 'em I wouldn't stand for it after what had happened; so a bunch o' us was on the way out here to put back the planks, when we heard shouts, and guessed somebody had fallen in. The rest dodged into the bushes, but I commenced to run this way. Then I met Will, here."

"And we got the ladder. He was only too willing to help," went on Will, plainly fully believing in the change of heart on the town bully's part.

"Say, that's all mighty interesting, but talk to me about it after you get a fellow out of this black hole. I thought I felt a snake right then. We used to kill 'em in here, too. Poke the ladder down, boys, please."

"That's a fact. As the drowning boy said: 'Save me first and scold me afterward.' Let me give you a hand, boys," remarked Frank.

"Hey! be careful there about getting too close to the edge. The whole bunch of you will be in on top of me if you don't look out. I had a crack on the head from a rock right then. And be careful how you poke that ladder down, or you may stick it through me like a lady's hatpin. Now I've got hold of the end, lower away, all."

So under the directions of the boy who was in the hole, and in a position to see how things lay, the single-pole ladder was placed in position.

"I'm coming up now, fellows; don't let the dirt crumble in on me," called Jerry.

"It does beat all how the adventures crowd you, old man. Here the rest of us just go along in an average way, and nothing happens to anybody to stir the blood. Hang it, I say it's hardly fair," remarked Frank, in pretended chagrin.

Jerry began to appear in view, clinging to the ladder, for it was a rather rickety affair, and threatening constantly to turn around, so that he had to fasten both knees and hands to the pole as he mounted.

"Keep her straight, Andy; you understand how hard it is to hustle up this old beam. I'm getting there all right, and don't you forget it," he kept saying, with a broad grin on his happy-go-lucky face as it came into plain view.

"Oh! Jerry, please hang there for just twenty seconds! You

don't know what a splendid picture you make. I'd give almost anything to snatch it off. Oblige me like a good fellow, won't you, please?" shouted Will, waving his hands entreatingly.

"Talk to me about nerve! You beat all creation. I'm holding on by the skin of my teeth, and you want me to wait till you get your measly old camera adjusted, and snap me off in this ignoble position. Well, I'm waiting, but it's to get my second wind, and not to oblige a crank," gasped Jerry.

"Oh! thank you, Jerry, thank you. It will only take a few seconds, I'm sure, and the result will be a constant source of delight to every member of the club."

"Yes, I've no doubt they'll go into spasms of laughter every time they look at the human ape hanging to his limb. Hurry up, plague take it; I'm getting weary of posing to suit your convenience. Why don't he, come back and finish? I declare if I can stand this any longer. I tell you I'm coming up, Will - picture or no picture."

"Here he comes; just hang on a bit longer," said Frank, soothingly.

Will came dashing up, showing the most intense excitement. His eyes fairly bulged from his head, and he was quivering all over.

"What ails you, man; are you sick?" demanded Frank, in real alarm.

"Sick? No, but I'm broken-hearted, that's what. It's gone!" shouted the other, wringing his hands, "some wretch has stolen my camera, and films!"

CHAPTER XXII

"LOOK PLEASANT, PLEASE!"

"What's that?" exclaimed Andy Lasher, jumping up from the side of Frank, where he had dropped to lend Jerry a helping hand.

"My camera's stolen! I placed it carefully behind that tree so nobody could step on it, and now the whole thing's disappeared!" said Will, almost choking with deep emotion.

"I bet that's the work of Pet Peters and the other fellows!" exclaimed Andy, his freckled face showing dark signs of anger.

"Hey, don't forget about me!" bellowed a voice from the depths; "the blooming old pole turned round then, and I slipped back five feet. Hold her steady, you fellows, and give me a chance to climb out!"

"That's a fact. Come along, Jerry," said Frank.

So the imprisoned one crawled out, only too glad to once more plant his feet on solid ground.

"Talk to me about your trapeze acts, and your parachute drops, I guess I know all the sensations. And let me tell you I don't hanker after any more of the same kind. Now, what's all this row about your black box, Will?" cried Jerry, as he felt of his various joints to make sure he was all sound.

"It's been hooked while we were getting you out. That Pet Peters has made way with it. Oh! if he ever tears open the package that contains my beloved films, I'm just ruined. All my work for nothing; and they can never be replaced again."

"We'll get 'em, don't you fear," exploded Andy. "I'll run back to camp right away, and make him give 'em up."

"If you only would, I'd be ever so much obliged, Andy. Three dozen, yes, four now, of the finest scenes a fellow ever could take. Why, some of them are *immense*!"

"I suppose you are referring now to that one where that yellow dog was chasing me around the tree; but I wouldn't die of grief if posterity never got a squint at that picture," said Jerry, shaking his head.

"Please start now," urged Will; "for they will be opening the package just for spite. One little bit of daylight and the whole thing will be ruined. And from what I know of Pet Peters, I believe he'd do it."

"I just reckon he would, now. All right, I'm off," said Andy.

"Wait, and we'll go with you," declared Frank, quietly.

"I can do it just as well alone; still, perhaps it is good to have you fellers along. But we must run," Andy observed.

"We can do it. Come on, boys!" cried Frank

They started off through the timber, even Jerry keeping up a rattling pace, although somewhat out of breath.

"Better not talk," admonished Andy, when Will manifested a disposition to continue his doleful wails about his terrible loss.

"That's good advice, Will. If you hope to recover your property, better keep a padlock on your lips just now. Besides, you need all your wind," remarked Frank.

They ran on.

The trail was crooked, but kept drawing nearer the lake all the while.

"Just a few minutes more," panted Andy at length.

And when less than that time had passed they could catch glimpses of the cabin in which he and his crowd had taken up their quarters, after being forestalled by the outdoor chums in the race for the hemlock camp.

Andy said nothing, but the manner in which he put his fingers on his lips as he turned his head, was indicative of silence.

He led them forward in such a way that the cabin stood between them and the spot where several boys seemed to have clustered, interested in something.

When they looked around the corner of the hut they counted five in the bunch. It was Pet Peters, a tall, raw-boned lad, who was swinging the camera to and fro in triumph, while he held up the waterproof package in which Will kept the rolls of films that had been exposed, awaiting the time when he could develop the same.

"Say, but won't them sissies be hoppin' mad w'en they sees it gone?" he was saying, with a grin; "an' we can keep it as long as we wanter."

"What's he got in the black bag, Pet?" demanded one of the others.

"Don't know, but we'll soon find out," grunted the leader of the group, looking around for a place to lay the camera down while he applied himself to the task of opening the tied-up package.

"I bet it's films he's used; I know, because I got a bull's-eye camera to home," exclaimed another chap, pressing forward eagerly.

"Who was it tumbled into the old mine shaft?" asked Pet, as he dug at the knot with which the cord was fastened.

"Don't know for sure, but I kinder think it must a-been Jerry Wallington. I seen that Frank and Will along with Andy," replied a third, quickly.

"Glad of it. Andy says as how he's under obligations to Jerry, but fur me I don't take any stock in that sorter thing. He jest couldn't let a feller lie there and die under that tree. It sarves Andy right because he wanted to cover up the old shaft again afore any purty boy fell down in it and skinned his nose. Say, how d'ye 'spose they ever found that ladder agin after we hid it?"

"'Course Andy got it for 'em. He oughter left the kid in the hole all night. Hope he's bunged up good and hard by the tumble," came from another.

"Looky here, Pet, ye know what ye're doin', I 'spect?" asked the one who had but a minute before owned to having a camera at home.

"Tryin' to open this pesky little package, all right," answered the other.

"But if it has them films inside ye'll ruin the hull bunch if ye lets daylight in on 'em. Undo the rolls that is wrapped each in black paper, and the picters is gone just as quick as that," and he snapped his fingers.

"What do I care? Sarves them right for takin' our camp away. For two cents I'd throw the hull business into the lake, and let her swim," growled Pet, who did not seem to be making much progress in his feat of untying the binding cord.

Frank could feel Will quiver with emotion as he pressed against him. The very thought of his beloved camera and those invaluable films floating on the water filled the boy with unutterable anguish. He even groaned, though the fact that the conspirators were so busily engaged, and talking in the bargain, prevented them from hearing the suspicious sound.

"Andy was a-helpin' 'em," declared one of the group, as though that fact might constitute a crime in his eyes.

"'Course; what more could ye expect arter the way he got us to go out with him to cover up that hole again? Andy's got religion, I reckon; leastways he ain't the same kind o' a feller he was," declared Pet.

"But he turned on you mighty quick, I noticed, an' sed as how he'd wipe up the ground with your remains if you jest didn't go along and help undo our work. He kin fight yet, even if he is changed," said the fellow who hung discreetly on the outskirts of the group, and who was evidently a devoted follower of the said Andy.

"Jest mind yer own business, Tom Somers, an' speak when yer spoken to. Guess I know that yer intendin' to stick to Andy through thick an' thin. But they ain't everybody feelin' that way, understand? If Andy he's a-goin' to turn on us and be chummy with that crowd, we ain't expectin' to stand it, see?" declared Pet, still struggling with the obstreperous knot.

"Them's my sentiments," observed another.

"Me, too, fellers?" declared a second.

"Yes, it's easy for ye to talk that ways when he ain't around; but let him give any one o' ye a single look an' it's eat dirt for the lot. Ain't I seen it done many a time? An' some day Andy's goin' to give Pet the time o' his life," the single faithful henchman kept saying.

"Oh, let up, Tom! Ain't any one o' ye got a knife? I can't never get this here knot untied. Hand it here, Billy. Now watch the fun, fellers," and as he spoke Pet opened a blade of the borrowed knife, and proceeded to lay it across the cord.

To judge by the way he sawed, that blade was too dull to cut butter.

"What d'ye call this thing, anyhow, Billy? One side's about as sharp as t'other, an' a feller couldn't commit suicide, if he tried to, with this frog-sticker."

"Try mine," said the fellow who owned a camera.

"Say, that's the cheese; it's got a edge all right. Now wouldn't little Willie Milton weep tears if he seen me a-doin' this to his property," and he bent down to sever the cord at one vicious blow.

Frank thought it high time to interfere.

These unscrupulous boys would not hesitate to destroy all the results of Will's hard labor, and, in fact, take the keenest delight in wringing his heart by so doing.

There was only one way apparently to stop the desecration and save those precious films from destruction. Although opposed to violence on general principles, still Frank knew very well that there are times when it becomes necessary for every one to stand up boldly for his rights.

He gave a nudge to Jerry which that worthy understood as a signal to be ready. Accordingly, Jerry raised his shotgun until he had covered the group in front of the cabin, and then waited for the word.

"Step out and hold them," whispered Frank, in his ear; and the four boys made a sudden appearance from behind the shack.

"Now, look pleasant, please, you fellows!" exclaimed Frank, as he made sure that he had his gun held on a line to cover the leader of the rebels in Andy Lasher's camp.

CHAPTER XXIII

MORE SIGNS OF TROUBLE

Pet Peters looked thoroughly frightened when he saw that he had been caught in the very act of opening another's property.

The truth of the matter was, he had been warned of late by the town authorities that on the very next occasion when caught taking things that did not belong to him, they would send him to the reform school.

"Don't you dare cut that string," said Frank, sternly; "or I won't answer for the consequences, Pet Peters."

The boy, with a scowl, threw the package down alongside the camera.

"There's yer old shebang. I ain't done it a speck o' harm. Was just kiddin', anyway. Knowed Will was around, an' jest wanted to make him squeal," he declared.

Of course it was a barefaced falsehood, as every one understood; but it seemed to be the natural thing for a fellow like Pet to say; he always squirmed out of a scrape that way, while Andy had at least shown a certain amount of boldness when caught.

"Will, step up and claim your property. If it has suffered any damage I'm going to make him pay for it, if I have to take him all the way back to Centerville," continued Frank.

Eagerly did the one addressed walk forward and pick up both camera and package of films. He was within three feet of those five boys, yet never a hand was outstretched to hinder him. They knew better. Those grim guns that bore upon them, and the angry faces of Jerry, Frank, yes, and Andy, impressed them deeply.

"Examine them, Will. Do you think either has been injured?" asked Frank.

"'Course they ain't. How could they be when I kerried 'em carefully. Them scratches was on ther camera afore I touched it, I'll swar to that!" exclaimed Pet, really alarmed by this time.

At which Andy grinned as if highly amused.

"I guess everything's safe, Frank. They stopped just in time. Another minute and the damage could not have been repaired," sang out the delighted Will, ready to almost dance with joy.

"Which is a lucky thing for them, then. Now, I don't know why we should hang out here much longer. We've got our own, and the air of this camp isn't quite as nice as I'd like. Shall we go, fellows?" asked Frank.

"Might as well," answered Jerry; "but before we do I think these chaps ought to be told that the sheriff promised to drop in and see us to-morrow; and that if there's any more of this humbug and annoyance tried, I'm going to ask him to take the whole bunch back to Centerville."

"And I promise to prefer a charge of malicious mischief against them, and an attempt to destroy property. Incendiarism is a crime, especially when life is placed in peril; and one of us might have been burned while we slept," added Frank, severely.

There were exclamations of alarm from the cowering boys. They had been intimidated by the guns of Jerry and his chum, but this new source of danger chilled their ardor wonderfully.

"I reckon we ain't goin' to try any more tricks, fellers. Thought we'd have a leetle fun out of this campin' business; but seein' as how ye take it so hard, we'd better draw off," muttered Pet, completely humbled.

"Yes, 'fun for the boys, but death to the frogs,' as the old story says. That sort of thing is too one-sided to suit me. Just play your jokes on each other, if you must amuse yourselves. We have our own way of extracting fun out of an outing. Well, come along, boys. And, Andy, thank you for helping get Jerry out of that hole."

He thrust out his hand to the other as he spoke, but Andy did not take it.

"Ain't got anything to do with the rest of ye; but Jerry he saved my life. I told him I was goin' to quit naggin' his crowd, an' so I am; but that don't mean I'm a turnin' a saint right away. Pet here is itchin' for a lickin', an' I got a good notion to 'commodate him."

Andy glared in the direction of his lieutenant, and it was plain to be seen that the spirit of warfare had not as yet been diminished in his bosom.

"Oh! well, have it out among yourselves, boys. As long as you leave us alone we won't bother you in the least, I give you my word," said Frank.

"Come on, you fellows," cried Will. "I'm anxious to get away from here. That Pet gave me the cold creeps when he came so near ruining my films. Ugh! me for the comforts of our own camp."

No one wanted to linger. Even Jerry was glad to turn his back on the old cabin and stalk away, with his gun over his arm.

"Say," called Will, over his shoulder, a few minutes later, as they were pushing through the woods and following the back trail.

"Well, what is it?" asked Jerry.

"We forgot something, boys,'' continued the other.

"What's that?" demanded Frank, coming to a stand.

"Why, when we were about it we ought to have demanded that they return Bluff's dandy, repeating shotgun," said Will.

Thereupon Frank broke out into a laugh and turned upon Jerry.

"Hear that, will you?" he remarked, as if tickled.

"Oh, rats! there's that blessed old gun bobbing up again. Will I ever hear the last of that machine?" exclaimed Jerry, shrugging his shoulders.

"Not till the ghost is laid, I suppose, Jerry," remarked Frank.

Jerry walked along at his side, still grumbling as if he had a difficult matter to solve and could hardly make up his mind.

Thus they came to the spot where the late catastrophe had taken place. The hole gaped at them in the trail.

"Say, this is a dangerous thing to leave uncovered. Some one else might fall in, perhaps one of that lumberman's kids if they happened to be playing hereabouts," remarked Frank, as they paused to look down once more into the dark depths.

"I wouldn't want my worst enemy to slip over that edge. My! but it was a queer sensation I had when falling. Let's cover the hole up again," remarked Jerry.

"If we can find the planks it would be a good idea," echoed Will.

They started a search immediately. When Andy and his followers had removed this cover, to substitute the frail one of slender sticks, quilted with dead leaves and a scattering of soil to deceive the eye, they could not have taken the boards far away.

"I'm dead sure they ain't in the hole," observed Jerry, as they hunted.

"Lucky for you they were not, as you might have broken a leg in striking hard planks instead of soft soil," remarked Frank.

"Here they are, boys!" sang out Will just then.

It took but a short time for them to carry the heavy planks back to the place, and cover up the hole the crazy gold-hunter had dug so many; years ago.

"Hope those sillies won't think to steal them off again. They might trap one of that lumberman's kids, and then the penitentiary for theirs, for sure," said Jerry, as he made sure the cover was secure on all sides.

"I rather think they've had a lesson this time, and won't be in any hurry to repeat the dose," laughed Frank; "come along boys."

Somehow Jerry seemed to lag behind the others.

"What's the matter with him?" asked Will, turning his thumb backward over his shoulder.

"Perhaps conscience is at work. Jerry has queer freaks, you know. Wait and see what develops," answered Frank, mysteriously, and, although his companion tried to get him to say more he absolutely declined.

It was a short time after this that they heard the boom of a gun.

"Hunters abroad, somewhere around. There goes a second, yes and a third. Game must be plenty where they are," remarked Will.

Frank did not reply, but the other saw that he was smiling as if his thoughts might be pleasant just then.

"I just bet he's thinking of my sister Violet," was what passed through the mind of the boy; but for once he was wrong.

They finally arrived at a point not a quarter of a mile from camp. Frank turned to see if Jerry was coming along, for he had not heard a sound from him.

"How about that venison you insisted on carrying? I hope you didn't leave it in that miserable pit, now, for I was calculating on having a feast for supper?" he asked, seeing that Jerry still plodded along close by.

"I've got it on my back all right, so don't worry, boys. And honest, now, come to think of it, I really believe the bundle saved me from a worse shock than I got. I landed on it, if you please. Don't know how it beat me down, but it served as a fine old buffer. I look on that blessed deer as my best friend."

"Listen!" exclaimed Will just then.

All of them could hear what seemed to be shouts ahead. They certainly came from the direction of the home camp.

"Now what do you suppose has happened there this time? Can't we ever take a little saunter through the woods without the camp being made the theater for all sorts of strange dramas

- wildcats, lunatics, and now what?" exclaimed Jerry.

"I think it would be just as well for us to sprint along and find out. That Toby seems fated to get into the queerest scrapes ever heard of. Here goes!" with which Frank began to run.

The others kept close at his heels, and as the outcries increased they even put on additional speed, bursting out of the timber to see as strange a spectacle as ever greeted the eyes of woodsmen returning to their camp.

CHAPTER XXIV

WHAT BLUFF DID

"Why, it's a bear!" exclaimed Jerry, as the three boys came to a standstill on the border of the camp.

"It sure is, and nothing less," admitted Frank, his face beginning to pucker up with the advance stages of a laugh.

"Oh! if I can only get my camera on him - what glorious luck!" breathed Will, as his trembling fingers worked to drag the little black box out of its cover.

The bear was busy just then, in fact, exceedingly engaged. He had taken to turning things over around the fire just as though some one had given him a sheriff's search warrant, and he meant to use it to the limit.

"He's hungry, all right; look at him getting away with the corn Uncle Toby was just going to cook for supper. Say, that must be the same old critter I interviewed while I was caged in that tree," said Jerry, tickled at the thought.

"What makes you think so?" demanded Frank.

"He's so curious and so persistent, you see. Besides, I don't believe there's another bear within ten miles of here. Oh! it's my old friend, you just bet. And that means I ought to have the privilege of slaying him."

"Don't be piggish, Jerry. Let some of the rest of us do something or other," remarked Frank, with a touch of satire in his voice.

He had his own gun handy, and meant to have a share in getting a supply of bear meat for the camp larder.

"Do you see Uncle Toby? I'll be blessed if he hasn't gone and made a ladder, and has used it to climb up in that tree yonder," declared Jerry, snickering.

"Sensible old Toby. If I had to make shift to be a monkey as often as he has, I think I'd have a ladder, too. Saves considerable trouble, you see, and the wear and tear on his clothes counts, too. But didn't we leave Bluff in camp - I don't see anything of our pard, do you, boys?"

A sharp "click" close to Frank's ear announced that Will was at his old tricks again. He had snapped off a view of the shaggy visitor squatted there with the open kettle between his paws, scooping up its juicy contents with evident relish. Canned corn was a treat that did not come his way every day, and Bruin meant to make the most of his opportunity.

"I thought I had a glimpse of something moving over there back of the tent, and it might be Bluff. I hope he don't try to shoo the old varmint off before we get a whack at him. I've only got bird-shot in my gun but at close quarters that ought to do as well as a bullet, eh, Frank?" asked Jerry, excited at the prospect.

"Wait I've a notion that you may be surprised yet. I've also a hunch, my boy, that there will be another claimant for the honors of this campaign. Sometimes surprises spring out of the very earth. Watch!" said Frank, laying a hand on the gun of his chum, as though impelling him to hold his fire.

Suddenly there was a loud bang!

The bear rolled over in a heap regardless of the congregated tinware that was consequently sent scurrying to the right and to the left.

"Who fired?" shouted the amazed Jerry.

"Look out, fellows, the old rascal's up again, and I guess I'd better get behind a tree with my camera!" exclaimed Will, suiting the action to the words with commendable rapidity.

Bang! went a second discharge at this juncture, and the bear now turning bit savagely at its hindquarters as though its wounds smarted severely.

Immediately a third discharge followed the others. Bruin had by this time apparently sighted the party from whom all these stinging cuts must have proceeded. He gave a roar of rage and lumbering awkwardly across the space started to try and climb a little tree just alongside one of the tents.

"It's Bluff, and he's up in that tree!" shouted Will, as he peeped around his own shelter, and took in the picture with another "click."

"But - he's got a gun!" stammered Jerry.

"Of course he has. Didn't he bring one with him? Perhaps a good fairy may have given him a tip as to where it could be found. There! he has fired again, and that time he missed, for the range was too close."

Frank, as he was speaking, commenced to advance into the open.

"Looky out, Marse Frank, he chaw yuh up, clean suah!" bawled Uncle Toby, from the crotch in the tree where his ladder had allowed him to reach. "Git up heah, honey, whah he can't reach yuh. Dat b'ar am ma-ad clar t'rough!"

"Four times he's shot - didn't I say he couldn't hit the side of a barn. Think of him carrying a Gatling gun," said Jerry.

"But he *has* hit him more than once. Look how the brute is bleeding, and just to think, Jerry, he's got two more chances. Those pump-guns don't seem so very bad in an emergency," laughed Frank, who seemed to be enjoying the little affair very much indeed.

"There goes one more; and the bear still lives. Talk to me about that, will you, if he didn't shoot its stub of a tail off that time! What next, I wonder? Why not execute the poor beast scientifically, and not murder him by inches?"

He moved his gun forward again as though bent on shooting. Frank, however, would not let him raise the weapon.

"Wait, I say; give Bluff one more chance. Make allowance for his excitement and his position while the bear is shaking that tree so. If he misses again we will both fire together and put an end to the comedy before it turns into a tragedy."

"That's what it will be if Bluff ever drops down into those claws. Why don't the duffer shoot? I can't stand it much longer, I tell you."

"Hold hard. I've no doubt he's waiting to get a good show, when the bear stops rocking that tree for a second. There now!"

A sixth roar drowned Frank's last words. This time Bluff must have steeled his nerves, and covered the side of the bear, for with the report the animal keeled over, made a vain attempt to get up again, gave a few kicks, and then lay still.

"Hurrah! Bluff has killed his bear!" yelled Frank, rushing forward, and swinging his hat excitedly.

"Come down here and stand over the fallen beast while I

immortalize you as the mightiest Nimrod of them all," called Will, rushing up with his camera ready to do the business with neatness and dispatch.

Jerry said nothing. He looked a bit dejected as he stood there and surveyed the dead bear. It was not envy that gripped his soul either, for Jerry was generous by nature. Something else had seized upon him, and Frank smiled as though satisfied with the way things had come out.

Bluff came scrambling down from his uncertain perch, looking wild.

"Is he really dead, fellows? Just to think that after all I did it with my new repeating shotgun! Ain't it a dandy, though? If Jerry hadn't gone to work and hid it away, I might have downed all the game that's come into this camp," he said, looking upon the black, hairy beast with a shudder, for he had had quite a severe fright while swaying to and fro with an angry bear beneath waiting for him to drop, like a ripe persimmon, as Jerry afterwards described it.

"Jerry?" shouted Will, in blank amazement.

"Yes, he stuck the gun in that long box over there. You remember his falling over it and bruising his shins. That was what gave him the miserable idea, I suppose. Anyway, he did it while the rest of us were out in the brush hunting for the fellow who threw those rocks into our camp," declared Bluff, scowling at the author of his woes.

Jerry laughed, a little forcedly it is true.

"I suppose I might as well own up, Bluff. I'm the guilty wretch, all right. The temptation came to me, and I did the job without thinking what it would mean to you. Honestly I've felt sore about it more than once since, and had just about made up my mind to confess, when by some accident, it seems, you found it. But you don't know it all. I hid the gun and then, when I went to see if it was safe, it was gone. I didn't know what to make of that, but fancied somebody else in camp had taken it. Then I commenced a search, and I found the gun down near that hole. I rather think some of the Lasher crowd came and took the gun, but I am not sure. After I found the gun I brought it to camp and put it in the box again. I take back some of the hard things I've been saying about that weapon. She can shoot, all right, and in the hands of an expert might, as I said, clean out all the game going."

"Frank told me to take another look around, just before you fellows left camp. I didn't have the heart to until a little while back, and was delighted to find the gun under those pieces of canvas in the box. It wasn't wet a bit in that hot old storm we had, either," continued Bluff again, as be contemplated his quarry, and then puffed out with honest pride.

"Say, was it you shooting a little while back?" asked Will, just then; "because we heard a lot of shots somewhere around."

"Why, yes, I got Uncle Toby to stand behind a tree, and throw up the wash basin half a dozen times while I banged away."

"Yes," said Frank, picking up the article in question, "and to judge from the holes you put through it we'll have to do without a basin during the remainder of our stay in camp. But how do you suppose this bear wandered into camp?"

"Reckons dat he jest smells de cawn, Marse Frank, w'en I opens up de can, an' by gorry, dat b'ar he can't resist de temptations to hab some. I seen him comin' foh me, an' I jest lets out a yell an' runs up dis yer safety ladder," remarked Toby, as he patted the article in question affectionately.

"We heard the yells, all right, and came running. Look here, Bluff, old man, you got your bear in spite of my playing that mean trick on you; are you going to call it quits, and be friends?" asked Jerry, holding out his hand.

"I - er - I don't know," stammered Bluff.

"I am just as sorry as I can be, Bluff, really I am, and I'd give the world if I hadn't played that trick. At first I was going to own up, but when you went off after the Lasher crowd it - well, I didn't see how I could do it. But after I got it back I hoped every hour that you would look into the box and discover the gun. Oh, say you'll forgive me!" added Jerry, pleadingly.

"Well, I feel a bit raw about it yet, but this is no time to show resentment, with such a glorious trophy at my feet. Yes, we'll call it quits, Jerry, only after this you might forget to sneer at a gun that happens to be different from yours."

"I agree, and that ends it," said Jerry, as he squeezed the other's hand.

CHAPTER XXV

BREAKING CAMP

And they had bear steak for supper.

Honestly, none of them thought a great deal of the treat, only that it seemed to be the proper thing for hunters to enjoy the results of their prowess with their guns.

Bluff was the happiest chap in camp, unless Will be excepted; he fondled that recovered gun almost the whole evening, and while Jerry winced every time he saw it, he dared not lift up his voice in protest after the great work which the so-called Gatling gun had done in the hands of a greenhorn.

Jerry with all his skill in the line of shooting had never been given the opportunity to kill a bear, and he felt that the time had gone by for him to class Bluff as a "come-on."

They spent a joyful evening, though, going over the exciting incidents of the last forty-eight hours again and again.

"And to think that we have only been up here a few days, boys. Why, if this sort of thing keeps on at this rate during our two weeks' stay, whatever in the world am I going to do for more films?" asked Will, plaintively.

"Keep the balance for especially good subjects," said Jerry, carelessly.

"Yes, but sometimes, you know, the best pictures are those you fail to get. Now, there was that one with you hanging to that ladder, I'll never get over my disappointment about losing that. Whenever anything of that sort crops up again, I hope nobody will steal my camera."

"Talk to me about dogged perseverance, this fellow certainly has 'em all beat to a frazzle," said Jerry, with an injured air, "I expect next he'll be proposing that we go back to that old shaft, and while I hang by my teeth to that blessed, shaky ladder, he will crack off a few views of the circus. Don't you dare propose that, or I'll forget my promise to be good, and begin to hide things again!"

"Oh! all right, I won't mention it, only it's a shame, that's what, when any fellow in these days refuses to put himself out a little just to oblige a friend, and interest posterity," grumbled Will.

They stayed up until quite late, singing songs of school and college life, and having a happy time. Not one among the four dreamed of the shadow that was even then hovering over Kamp Kill Kare.

There was no alarm that night, for which one and all felt grateful. This thing of being aroused out of a sound sleep to have the covers whipped off by a roaring gale may read all very nice, but the reality is quite a different matter. And when wild animals invade the peaceful camp it strikes one as very funny in print, but is apt to bring about a chilly feeling when encountered in real life.

As usual, Frank was the first one up, and he soon had the camp astir with his cheery calls. The nipping, frosty air proclaimed that now the Fall had come in earnest, and that they would be glad after this to keep a fire burning during each night, for warmth.

As they sat about the blaze after breakfast, laying out plans for the day, the sound of a horse's neigh startled them.

"It's the sheriff, I reckon," said Jerry, as they jumped up.

And he had guessed correctly, for presently they saw a horseman appear, and as he came up he waved his hand in greeting.

"Sorry, boys, but I've got some bad news for you," he said.

"Anybody dead, or sick?" asked Frank, turning a bit pale.

"Oh, no, nothing of that sort, I'm glad to say. This concerns you fellows only?" was the quick reply of Mr. Dodd, the sheriff.

The four boys looked at one another with alarm.

"I bet I know what it is - the Head has concluded to start the school up under half a roof, and wants us to come back right away!" said Will, mournfully.

Mr. Dodd laughed aloud.

"Hit it the first slat out of the box, Will. And you've got to report to-morrow morning, so you must go back to-day sure. I saw some of your fathers, and they say the same, so there's no escape. Sorry to bring you bad news; but looks like you've been doing your share of game-getting in the short time you were here," nodding toward the bear that was hanging up, and the deerskin, as well as the pelt of the invading wildcat.

"Well, it's hard lines, sir, but I suppose we have to obey. But get off and have breakfast. Toby just loves to cook, you know. There's plenty of coffee left, and you can have your choice of bear steak, or venison," said Jerry, hospitably.

So the sheriff made himself at home. He even assisted the boys get their things together preparatory to moving back to town, before riding on further.

The motor-cycles had been securely packed away under the big fly all this time, and had not suffered at all from the rain. Indeed, the boys took good care to keep them well oiled, knowing the benefit of having such valuable pieces of mechanism in first-class order at all times.

Jerry went over to the farmer's and secured the horses and wagon. Then the work of dismantling Kamp Kill Kare began. They tried to appear gay, but every one of the boys had become attached to the place during their short stay, and felt badly over leaving these scenes with so much undone that they had planned for.

"Never mind, fellows, we're going to come again and again. This first camp of the Rod, Gun and Camera Club isn't going to be the last, by any means. And I guess we've learned a good many things on this trip," sang out Jerry, cheerily.

"That's true every day, with all of us. I'm learning all the time. And next year when we get under canvas we will have a lot of pleasant memories to look back to. Why, with Will's pictures to help out, the winter will be a constant feast of stories about the things that have happened to us up here," remarked Frank.

"I'd like to have seen more of old Jesse. He's just chock full of woods lore, and can give you all the points you want about animals and such. How are things getting on out there, fellows? Is the wagon pretty well loaded?" asked Jerry.

"Have the last tent packed away in ten minutes. Toby says he can drive all right, but we'll keep near by to lend him a hand if necessary. The road is some rough in places until we get on the pike."

Half an hour later the wagon moved away from the camp under the hemlocks. Uncle Toby looked back and grinned amiably as he noted his ladder of protection, and his friendly tree of refuge.

Each boy in turn started his machine by walking, then vaulted into the saddle, and began to move along the trail that led down to the lumber camps at the head of the lake.

No one said a word. In truth all were too full of emotion to speak, for they felt this sudden flitting more than they cared to admit.

A turn of the trail and no longer could they see the twin hemlocks under which the two khaki tents had stood. Frank had broken up many times in his camping experiences and knew just how it felt; but the sensation was new to the others. It was as if they had just lost a dear friend - as though something had gone out of their lives that could never be recovered again.

Now in advance of the trundling wagon, and anon bringing up the rear, they kept on until finally the opening at the lumber camp was gained. From now on their progress would be faster, and if they wished they could leave Toby to come along with the wagon while they opened up and made a speedy run for home.

Somehow no one seemed to care about doing that. The wagon held something that had been associated in their minds with the most delightful of times, and they felt as though they ought to continue to act as a guard of honor to the slow moving team.

"Cheer up, fellows," called Frank, seeing how gloomy his chums looked; "every one of us has good reason for feeling proud and satisfied, even if our vacation has been cut short. I know I'm glad I came. I've had just a glorious time!"

"And to think of the fine pictures I'll be developing to-night. Oh! don't I hope they turn out good, though. Frank, you promised to come around and help me with your advice. I wouldn't take a chance of spoiling those views for anything," said Will, beginning to brighten up at the thought.

"And sure, I ought to be satisfied, with a deer, four wild dogs, and part of a wildcat, too, as my portion," exclaimed Jerry, also smiling again.

"Well, what d'ye think of me then, me and the blessed old pump-gun you used to make so much fun about? A bear, a great big savage bear that was trying to shake me down out of that tree It's in the wagon, too, and all our folks are going to try how sharp their teeth are when they get to biting a genuine bear steak. I rather think I'm in this thing some, eh, fellows?" demanded Bluff, positively.

"Yes, I rather believe you lead the procession this time, Bluff. Go up ahead, and do the grand marshal act when we get near home. But, say what you will, boys, we did have glorious fun. I doubt whether any fellows ever had more adventures crowded into so short a time before. And we're all of the same mind, I take it, ready to try it again at the very first opportunity," said Frank.

And how they did try it again will be told in another book, to be called: The Outdoor Chums on the Lake; or, Lively Adventures on Wildcat Island." In that volume we shall meet all our young friends again, and likewise their enemies, and follow out the particulars of some decidedly thrilling happenings.

"Before we get into civilization again, let's give one last rousing cheer for good old Kamp Kill Kare," cried Jerry.

"Hurrah! hurrah! hurrah! tiger!" rang out four boyish voices; and then, waving an imaginary farewell to the pleasant camp under the hemlocks, the outdoor chums turned once more to the duties of school life.

George Eliot
George Gissing
George MacDonald
George Meredith
George Orwell
George Sylvester Viereck
George Tucker
George W. Cable
George Wharton James
Gertrude Atherton
Gordon Casserly
Grace E. King
Grace Gallatin
Grace Greenwood
Grant Allen
Guillermo A. Sherwell
Gulielma Zollinger
Gustav Flaubert
H. A. Cody
H. B. Irving
H.C. Bailey
H. G. Wells
H. H. Munro
H. Irving Hancock
H. Rider Haggard
H. W. C. Davis
Haldeman Julius
Hall Caine
Hamilton Wright Mabie
Hans Christian Andersen
Harold Avery
Harold McGrath
Harriet Beecher Stowe
Harry Castlemon
Harry Coghill
Harry Houidini
Hayden Carruth
Helent Hunt Jackson
Helen Nicolay
Hendrik Conscience
Hendy David Thoreau
Henri Barbusse
Henrik Ibsen
Henry Adams
Henry Ford
Henry Frost
Henry James
Henry Jones Ford
Henry Seton Merriman
Henry W Longfellow
Herbert A. Giles
Herbert Carter
Herbert N. Casson
Herman Hesse
Hildegard G. Frey
Homer
Honore De Balzac
Horace B. Day
Horace Walpole
Horatio Alger Jr.
Howard Pyle
Howard R. Garis
Hugh Lofting
Hugh Walpole
Humphry Ward
Ian Maclaren
Inez Haynes Gillmore
Irving Bacheller
Isabel Hornibrook
Israel Abrahams
Ivan Turgenev
J.G.Austin
J. Henri Fabre
J. M. Barrie
J. Macdonald Oxley
J. S. Fletcher
J. S. Knowles
J. Storer Clouston
Jack London
Jacob Abbott
James Allen
James Andrews
James Baldwin
James Branch Cabell
James DeMille
James Joyce
James Lane Allen
James Lane Allen
James Oliver Curwood
James Oppenheim
James Otis
James R. Driscoll
Jane Austen
Jane L. Stewart
Janet Aldridge
Jens Peter Jacobsen
Jerome K. Jerome
John Burroughs
John Cournos
John F. Kennedy
John Gay
John Glasworthy
John Habberton
John Joy Bell
John Kendrick Bangs
John Milton
John Philip Sousa
Jonas Lauritz Idemil Lie
Jonathan Swift
Joseph A. Altsheler
Joseph Carey
Joseph Conrad
Joseph E. Badger Jr
Joseph Hergesheimer
Joseph Jacobs
Jules Vernes
Julian Hawthrone
Julie A Lippmann
Justin Huntly McCarthy
Kakuzo Okakura
Kenneth Grahame
Kenneth McGaffey
Kate Langley Bosher
Kate Langley Bosher
Katherine Cecil Thurston
Katherine Stokes
L. A. Abbot
L. T. Meade
L. Frank Baum
Latta Griswold
Laura Dent Crane
Laura Lee Hope
Laurence Housman
Lawrence Beasley
Leo Tolstoy
Leonid Andreyev
Lewis Carroll
Lewis Sperry Chafer
Lilian Bell
Lloyd Osbourne
Louis Hughes
Louis Tracy
Louisa May Alcott
Lucy Fitch Perkins
Lucy Maud Montgomery
Luther Benson
Lydia Miller Middleton
Lyndon Orr
M. Corvus
M. H. Adams
Margaret E. Sangster
Margret Howth
Margaret Vandercook

Margret Penrose
Maria Edgeworth
Maria Thompson Daviess
Mariano Azuela
Marion Polk Angellotti
Mark Overton
Mark Twain
Mary Austin
Mary Catherine Crowley
Mary Cole
Mary Hastings Bradley
Mary Roberts Rinehart
Mary Rowlandson
M. Wollstonecraft Shelley
Maud Lindsay
Max Beerbohm
Myra Kelly
Nathaniel Hawthrone
Nicolo Machiavelli
O. F. Walton
Oscar Wilde
Owen Johnson
P.G. Wodehouse
Paul and Mabel Thorne
Paul G. Tomlinson
Paul Severing
Percy Brebner
Peter B. Kyne
Plato
R. Derby Holmes
R. L. Stevenson
R. S. Ball
Rabindranath Tagore
Rahul Alvares
Ralph Bonehill
Ralph Henry Barbour
Ralph Victor
Ralph Waldo Emmerson
Rene Descartes
Rex Beach
Rex E. Beach
Richard Harding Davis
Richard Jefferies
Richard Le Gallienne
Robert Barr
Robert Frost
Robert Gordon Anderson
Robert L. Drake
Robert Lansing
Robert Lynd
Robert Michael Ballantyne
Robert W. Chambers
Rosa Nouchette Carey
Rudyard Kipling
Samuel B. Allison
Samuel Hopkins Adams
Sarah Bernhardt
Sarah C. Hallowell
Selma Lagerlof
Sherwood Anderson
Sigmund Freud
Standish O'Grady
Stanley Weyman
Stella Benson
Stella M. Francis
Stephen Crane
Stewart Edward White
Stijn Streuvels
Swami Abhedananda
Swami Parmananda
T. S. Ackland
T. S. Arthur
The Princess Der Ling
Thomas A. Janvier
Thomas A Kempis
Thomas Anderton
Thomas Bailey Aldrich
Thomas Bulfinch
Thomas De Quincey
Thomas Dixon
Thomas H. Huxley
Thomas Hardy
Thomas More
Thornton W. Burgess
U. S. Grant
Valentine Williams
Various Authors
Vaughan Kester
Victor Appleton
Victoria Cross
Virginia Woolf
Wadsworth Camp
Walter Camp
Walter Scott
Washington Irving
Wilbur Lawton
Wilkie Collins
Willa Cather
Willard F. Baker
William Dean Howells
William le Queux
W. Makepeace Thackeray
William W. Walter
William Shakespeare
Winston Churchill
Yei Theodora Ozaki
Yogi Ramacharaka
Young E. Allison
Zane Grey

www.ingramcontent.com/pod-product-compliance
Lightning Source LLC
LaVergne TN
LVHW090607110826
845146LV00001B/291

* 9 7 8 1 4 2 1 8 2 4 4 9 9 *